*How
Can I Find You,
God?*

Reading

*Whosoever shall read this writing, and shew
me the interpretation thereof, shall be clothed
with scarlet, and have a chain of gold about his neck.*

Daniel 5:7

How Can I Find You, God?

MARJORIE HOLMES

Illustrated by Betty Fraser

DOUBLEDAY & COMPANY, INC.
GARDEN CITY, NEW YORK
1975

All biblical quotations are from the King James Version unless otherwise noted.

Grateful acknowledgment is made to Hodder & Stoughton, Ltd., for permission to use excerpts from *The Reality of the Religious Life,* by Henry Bett.

First Edition
ISBN: 0-385-04437-2
Library of Congress Catalog Card Number 74–25107
Copyright © 1975 by Marjorie Holmes Mighell
All Rights Reserved
Printed in the United States of America

CONTENTS

For Margaret Mighell Rosendahl

Introduction

People are hungry for God. We are trying to find him. Sex trips, drug trips, mind trips, the whole sensitivity bag, are manifestations. The God Is Dead movement was nothing but a crash program to demonstrate how deep and fierce is this hunger to relate in a meaningful way to a meaningful Creator.

This hunger is innate. Man is born with an insatiable curiosity about the source of his own being. It is reflected in the earliest questions of children, who accept God as a living reality. (They ask but they don't *doubt*.) Likewise primitive people, or often the very poor or the uneducated. There is a kind of divine simplicity about their faith. As we become more civilized, affluent, intellectual, God gets "complicated out." Life is too full, too crowded; in the struggle for mere survival or success and happiness on human terms, we are weaned away from God, many times abandon him altogether.

Yet the *hunger* remains. We are pursued as by Francis Thompson's *Hound of Heaven*. And often the greater the material and intellectual achievements, the more we are haunted by this sense of vacancy, this need for spiritual fulfillment. We begin to sense that if there is no reason for being born and nothing to anticipate after death, then there is no reason for our achievements, no reason to exist or even want to see the world go on. We have no answers for our children. Why *not* seek self-annihilation through drugs, or otherwise?

I believe that God will not let go of his most precious creation so easily. It is his footsteps we feel behind us, his hand on our heart, his voice that rouses us in the night. His hunger for us is as intense as our secret hunger for him. He wants us to find our way back.

This book points out some of the paths that have helped me find God again.

How Can I Find You, God?

How can I find you, God? How can I track you down and take you into my life and be one with you in peace and joy always? How can I make you mine?

I am a busy wife and mother. I have children and grandchildren, a house to keep, a husband to please, a job in which I must produce. There are many demands upon my time. . . . And I am not alone in this. I am but one of millions of people, men as well as women, wanting to know you better, wanting to feel your presence, wanting to turn to you for comfort or help, but so busy, so frenziedly busy, with almost no time or place of peace or privacy in which to meet you, reach out to you in meditation or prayer.

You have become a stranger to us. The God that we knew as children, loved and trusted as children, got lost somewhere along the way. Many of us lost you in college, suffering the shock of intellectualism for the first time. Many of us lost you to the cynics, the scoffers, the would-be sophisticates.

Many of us lost you through trouble and disappointments, prayers that didn't seem to be answered, and so we shook our fists in your face and turned away. Or we lost you through our very good fortunes, wealth, success (who needs you?). We even lost you, some of us, through churches that put up too many barriers between us. We lost you in so many ways, too numerous to count.

But I think most of us lost you through sheer indifference. The indifference that comes with giving everything else priority. Living demands priority, responsibilities demand priority. We've been too busy for you, God, we've gotten out of the habit of you.

Now we want you back. Timorously, belatedly, a little ashamed of ourselves, we're trying to find you again, inviting you back. Life is too empty without you. Life is too futile and meaningless without

*you. Life has no flavor. We're anxious without knowing why. We're
lonely. We need something to fill the void—and it must be you.*

*Please come back, God. Hear our voices, direct our groping,
cut through this clutter and become a part of us again. Become as
real to us as you were when we were children; as simple, powerful,
loving, reassuring. Help us to find you, show us the ways to reach
you.*

People

I know that I am a person and that it is persons—
especially a few particular persons—not things, who have
influenced me and had a power in my life.

Forbes Robinson

The Old Man

I am looking for God, I am looking for God in people. I scan their faces seeking some sign of his presence. If the kingdom of God is truly within us then he must dwell there, and it will show in a smile, the eyes, the touch of a hand. Yet who has ever truly seen God? And is my measure too simple?

We are told that we are made in his image. Yet the image we see is so often ugly. Warped, decrepit, misshapen; or distorted by slyness, egotism, evil and greed. No, no, if I seek such proof of the presence of God, I will be disappointed.

Yet now and then God sings out from a face, the very radiance and power of God. . . . An old colored man on a bench in a railroad station, tall, lean, gentle, snowy-haired, serene. And emanating God. It shone from those eyes, so ancient and wise in the narrow, wrinkled face; it was in the tenderness and sweetness of the long full lips. Intensely, undeniably, I felt it; in a wave of almost intolerable love and recognition I felt it. Here was a man who had known much suffering but only been purified by it, who had never lost hold of the hand of God.

And as we chatted about simple things—the sunshine, friendships, reunions and partings—I heard God in his voice as well. And he smiled at my little girl, who said she was thirsty. And as he rose in his threadbare but immaculate black suit, and led her to the water fountain and lifted her up to drink, I was touched and humbled and filled with awe, for here was some part of God in action. And when we left him I felt cleansed and blessed, for I knew I had been in the presence of a man who manifested God.

And there have been others. Rare moments when the goodness of God looks straight into your heart from a pair of eyes and says: "I am here. Follow me." A very great woman looked at me like that once and I couldn't bear it. I wasn't ready. I turned away.

But these things happen without our seeking. You can't track God down on the streets, he comes when you're not looking, he takes you by surprise. Yet I have found, or have at least come closer to finding, God through people.

Many people.

Parents

Parents are the first people we know. When we are babies, *they* are God to us. And when we begin to question the mystery of our being upon this marvelous planet, if they are people of God they introduce us to him, lead the way. Although actually young children don't need an introduction, their knowledge of God is innate. They love and accept God as passionately and instinctively as they love a flower.

But as we mature, this simple, instinctive acceptance gets crowded out. We begin to question the values of our parents, we rebel. And we begin to question and to rebel against God. We don't want authority any more; we want to be independent, to stride forth into the world unencumbered by things we think we've outgrown; we want to make it on our own.

Yet parents are the source of that first conscious knowledge of God. And before that the very source of self. It's impossible to reject parents without rejecting a vital part of oneself. Maybe that's why the hurt goes so deep on both sides when the cleavage comes; why the ache persists so long even after the early wounds are healed. And maybe that's why the heart that has once felt close to God aches so mysteriously after it has turned away. We want to go back, we "want to go home." Yet we don't want to revert to being little kids again, taking our faith much as we once took food and support and other comforts from our elders. We want it to be significant and exciting, something we've found and claimed alone. . . . But how? How?

So we grope and stumble along. . . . And all the while, back there, are the parents, often puzzled and troubled about us, but unable to help. Except by just being themselves, living what they believe. And helping, often more than any of us realize, by the memories of what they were.

Mother

We are inclined to idealize mothers, especially after they're gone. How can I write of mine honestly and fairly, without sentimentality, as I seek to weigh her influence on my search?

Mother was no angel, she was a very human woman, beset by many trials and riddled by many faults. But she was the most compassionate person I ever knew, and she had faith. No matter how dire the circumstances or hopeless the future seemed, she clung stubbornly, almost exasperatingly, to her God.

In my callow need to criticize I used to think it was the church organization that held her. And she did take delight in all its activities, the ladies' aid and bake sales, the suppers and bazaars. (What's wrong with that? I ask myself now. God knows we all need fellowship, and if it filled a social need why not?) And she gave of herself, how much she gave. She played the organ, directed the choir, taught Sunday school for nearly fifty years. But it was so much more than that. She loved that church and she loved the people and she loved God.

And the most fervent, high-sounding arguments failed to shake her. I could quote Kierkegaard, she could quote Christ. I could "prove" religion a myth by marshaling sophomore science. She would smile rather wistfully and shake her head and say, "Well, I can't argue with you, but ask your scientist to create a rose."

I regret the pain that my apostasy caused my mother, but there is no use grieving over it now. I've asked forgiveness, and tried to forgive myself. But I honestly don't think the questioning is a sin to be forgiven (God gave us minds to use). The sin, if any, is the sheer arrogance of trying to override somebody else's ideals, wreck faith, destroy something that the other holds sacred, that gives another life meaning.

How cruelly selfish, because we do this for almost only one reason, especially in the case of parents: To humble them, to vaunt our superiority.

But then youth is often cruel. . . .

Please help me to remember that, God, when my own children turn their ruthless superiority on me.

Dad

What did I learn about God from my father? What can I learn that will help me even now?

I didn't learn much directly, for he had come from God-scorning people and he wasn't a churchgoing man. At least not of his own volition, he went only to please Mother. He didn't even join for many years, refusing to be a hypocrite, and it was hard for him to give up swearing when he finally did.

It was his only vice. He didn't drink, was never untrue to his wife. He never cheated another man, though he was cheated often because he was so trusting. . . . He was a witty, gutsy, jovial, resourceful, imaginative, gay little man who adored his family, worked hard for them without complaint, and emptied his pockets for them, usually without thanks. Despite his perennial good humor, he sat sometimes with a baffled and rather forlorn expression, as if gazing upon the ruins of his many bright and truly valid dreams. . . .

This dad, this earthy earthly father . . . looking back I find more pointers toward God in him than I realized. He was not complex, he was never remote. He was never too busy to listen to us. And though he sometimes got mad and yelled and was stern and we thought him unfair, we found out he wasn't. He was quick to forgive and he never held a grudge.

He loved us, was concerned about us, and was proud of us. He never let any of us down, not once. . . .

What more can anyone ask of a father? And if this is the nature of a good earthly father, why shouldn't the father of us all be just as easy to know and to trust?

They've been gone quite a while now, Lord, both Mother and Dad. I can't go to them and say, "Help me, I'm trying to find God." But now that their lives are completed and mine is well advanced I can perhaps get their answer more clearly than if they spoke to me in person. All that they were testifies to your nearness and reality.

Parents. Good parents or even bad parents. They are the source of self, and beyond them is the source of the very source. Follow that line far enough and one comes to no other force or source than God. . . . I want to be a good parent to my children, and to make them aware of the wonder of a loving Creator; but even if I fail, because I lived and bore them I am still their life line to a mystery so marvelous that it takes the breath away. To be *alive* and able to think about it is surely to touch the truth of God.

Children

Children can help us to find God.

The birth of a child (what a miracle) . . . The death of a child (how can any parent bear this heartbreak without the assurance that he will see his child again, its life will go on?).

And a youngster asking, "Where did I come from?" "Who made that tree?" "Why do we have stars?" How can we answer their questions without saying, even when we don't understand it ourselves: "God."

And their eagerness to learn about Jesus, to go to Sunday school. Often reluctantly, dreading it, parents dutifully take them—and find beauty there and kindred spirits, and a reawakening of their own interests and hungerings.

Or an older child will discover God on his own and bring the good news home. And if they're any kind of parents at all, they will at least listen, they won't discourage him. Sometimes his sheer enthusiasm prevails: they, too, are caught up by the wonder of God and are swept along.

Sometimes deep trouble with a child brings us up sharp, face to face with God. "Spare him, spare us . . . oh, forgive us for our neglect and disbelief, help us, God!"

And just to raise children—the sheer responsibility it entails. How can we do it without a strength beyond our own, a wisdom beyond our own? Sometimes scared, sometimes trusting, sometimes in joy, sometimes in desperation, we reach out and say, "Where are you? I need you, help me to find you, God."

Dear God, whenever a child comes to me with questions, help me to find the answers; speak through me, don't let me falter and fail him. And when a child begs, "Come with me!" let me go. And when a child says to me, "It's so wonderful—I've found God!" don't let me be indifferent or superior or amused; let me rejoice with him, let me share the wonder. . . . And don't let me call on you only in times of desperate need.

Keep close to me always as I try to raise my children. Be real to me, be real to me. Be a part of my life, and of theirs.

"I Would Die for It"

Brief contacts with people whose faith is strong can help us to find God.

I met this man at a writers' conference and we became good friends for several days. We spoke at length about many things. He was a devout Catholic and he told me what the Sacrament meant to him. "When I go to the altar and take the wafer, I become one with Christ, completely, in every way. I can't describe what I feel except that it's beyond any joy I've ever experienced. *I would die for it.*"

I believed him. Awed and incredulous, I still believed him. And his words haunted me.

The Waitress

Jeanette Yee is a waitress in the coffee shop of a big busy medical building in Washington, D.C., and she often tells this story to patients eating there.

She hadn't been to church since childhood. But after a fall on the ice she had a cerebral hemorrhage; and while still unconscious the nurse heard her say, "I'm going to die and I don't know how to pray." The nurse ran out and brought in a minister to comfort her.

Not long after, she contracted both rheumatoid arthritis and diabetes, so severely she was put on heavy medication and there were times when the doctors despaired. Yet something else had begun to work in her. "I still didn't go to church, but when I'd see the doctor I'd tell him, 'One of these days Jesus is going to heal me.' He didn't believe me, of course; and I was getting so bad he told my son I'd soon have to go to the hospital or I wouldn't survive."

Then one day a lady called her from Christ Church. Its pastor, McArthur Jollay, said he felt impelled to pray for her. "So I went to him, and he anointed my head and prayed for God to heal me, and it was the most fantastic thing. There was heat that poured down from my head to my toes; it was as if it was coming out of the pores of my skin in waves. The healing was instantaneous. I knew it!

"And I went home where I heard a voice say clearly, 'Throw that medicine away. From this day forth you won't need it. My grace is sufficient.' And it is! That was eight years ago, and I haven't taken a pill since or had a sick day."

At first her doctor was shocked, incredulous; but when he ran tests he was forced to confirm her cure. Since then Jeanette has seen and participated in other miracles of healing; and no day passes that she doesn't witness to someone going to or from a hospital: "You might also try God."

People Need Each Other

People need each other so much, God. We need you, but we need each other, too. In a very human sense we need each other.

You don't want us to be lonely, you give us people, many people (too many sometimes!). And out of the many you lead us to the few, the precious few we can really talk to.

And as we talk about things that really matter—troubles, hopes, confidences, things we wouldn't dare share with anyone else—we go deeper. With a friend like this, who loves and understands us, we begin to talk about life and its meaning.

We talk about you.

Sometimes we discover you together. Two children groping, stumbling upon exciting aspects of your nature we couldn't have found alone. And we look at each other amazed and marveling.

Or one of us will lead the other. The wiser one (not necessarily the older) who has known you longer and more constantly, or more vividly experienced you . . . And this is so wonderful, to have a friend, man or woman, who walks confidently on his or her spiritual journey and says, "Come on, don't be afraid." Who, without preaching or inferring superiority, will help to clear the path and guide the way.

I have such a friend, Lord. I have several such friends. How can I ever thank you enough for them? They are surely a part of your plan for drawing each of us back to you.

"I Saw Your Light"

She rang the doorbell unexpectedly one night, a woman I'd known casually at PTA. Young, vigorous, dark-eyed, vibrant, the mother of four boys.

"I just had to stop," she told me, "I was coming home from the library and I saw your light. I checked out this book by Paul

Tournier for the third time and suddenly it seemed selfish to keep it another month—maybe you'd like to read it?"

I glanced at it and didn't particularly want to; I was so busy and had a lot of reading already piled up. But it seemed so nice of her I accepted the offer. And suddenly we began to talk about books and I made coffee and she called home to be sure her husband had the boys in hand, and we talked till midnight.

I don't remember much of what we discussed, only that here was someone I could relate to intellectually. And spiritually! For the first time in years—spiritually. Her faith sang and shone and radiated from her, and she told me about it because I asked. She was not out to convert me to anything, certainly that was not why she had called. But she had sensed, in that way that highly perceptive and intelligent people often do, that there was something in me lost and groping. Something that she could perhaps help me find.

Mainly she awoke me to my own needs. God-haunted, God-hounded, but always scoffing and turning away because God seemed to me another taskmaster who would rout me out of bed Sunday morning when I wanted to sleep, who'd insist that I pray when I didn't know how. Who'd make me feel guiltier than I already did because of yelling at the children or envying a neighbor or holding a grudge, all my persistent daily sins and omissions, as well as fantasies of more dramatic ones.

As we talked that night and on later occasions, she made me see this was stupid and silly. "You've set up God as your mortal enemy, instead of someone who can help." She, too, was human and guilty of practically everything I was. "But knowing he loves you anyway and forgives you is such a relief. You really don't feel so *unforgivably* guilty when you slip. It's this self-punishment, the self-berating that is so bad. I'm much harder on myself than God is. Left to myself I'm hopeless, but with God there's a chance for me. And somehow with this knowledge it gets better. You do simply become a better person, easier to live with. At least you keep trying, and with some purpose; you don't just keep floundering in your wretchedness."

I'm sure we had other conversations much more searching and profound; I even wrote some of them down. But I don't remember them. Those words, however, I never forgot. Subtly but strongly they altered my image of God. What's more—they worked!

Not long after that we moved, and except for an occasional phone call we lost touch.

I had taken the book back to the library only half read, for I found Tournier pretty hard going right then. But I often think of its title: *The Meaning of Persons.*

She had demonstrated that meaning.

One Woman's Way

Another friend, very close to me. As close now as my own sister . . .

When I first knew and enjoyed her I had no idea that she had been on a long desperate search herself, and had finally found God. She needed him, for there was almost nobody else to turn to. Married to a Jewish atheist, with a dominating live-in mother-in-law and six children, she had been like a child herself. The oldest child in the nursery, but locked in and scared to try to break out.

"I couldn't even pray, I'd forgotten how, and the Bible didn't make sense any more. I tried to go to church, but it was hard when even the kids were encouraged to make fun of me. Then one day I went to an art gallery where an artist friend was having an opening. It was the first place I'd been in ages, I had hardly any clothes and just couldn't face people, but something propelled me there that day, and it was like an escape from prison.

"And the woman in charge of the show came up and talked to me about going to work for them and I said, 'Yes, yes, when do I start?' And she said, 'Right now, take charge of the guest book.' She was a very sensitive woman and she must have seen that I needed the freedom as much as the money, which certainly wasn't much. But even something more, I was starving for something more that she could give me.

"In the days that followed we talked and I was always so amazed—that anyone so cultured and sophisticated could be so serene and happy in her religion. It was as if she were introducing me to a good friend who could actually help me out of my misery, somebody vaguely familiar whom I'd met before but been afraid to pursue. And one day she asked, 'Are you ready to receive the Baptism in the Holy Spirit?' and I said, 'Yes, yes,' just as spontaneously as I had accepted her offer of the job. And she put her hands on me and prayed, and a great joy and peace went through me and when I went home I was really floating. Praying came easily after that, it was as if I'd fallen in love with God and he, God, was assuring me that somebody really loved me.

"And I was free! Not merely getting out of the house, although that was very important, the beginning—but free inside. Free to love my mother-in-law instead of resenting her tyranny. Free to love my husband, even though he was to blame for keeping her there and letting her intimidate me. Nobody *could* intimidate me any more, because of this new knowledge of the presence of God and its incredible freedom. And they just could not understand it."

Baffled, and perhaps feeling robbed of a victim, the mother-in-law moved out. "But that was best for her, too. She was freed of her entanglements with *us*. She made a life of her own and stood on her own feet for the first time." There were continuing problems, however, with money, gambling debts, infidelity. It was a fiercer kind of hell, a deeper descent into the pit; but my friend could take it. She had become her own person now, and she had an ally.

When our paths finally crossed, she had come a long way. Brilliant, pretty, witty, joyful, she had become almost the sole support of her family. And through gifts she hadn't even realized she had. "When God frees you, it doesn't mean you're *in* free. He makes even more demands on you, he shows you how much more you're capable of, and he expects you to produce. It's not easy by any means, but it's so much better than to feel trapped and alienated and lost."

I respect her, admire her, love her so much, God. She has helped me find you, just as she was led to you through the woman in the gallery that day.

Thank you that when we really need it, you will always send someone to help us find our way.

The Young Girl

She spoke for us one Sunday, a beautiful girl who had lived for three years in a Christian commune. A little ripple of apprehension could be felt. . . . Here was antiestablishment youth, challenging everything most of us represented.

Yet her voice was like music, her eyes shone, saying: "Jesus hated hypocrisy. He wanted each Christian to be a living model of the good news. Ours is a place where people can learn that kind of Christianity—to witness to the world that Jesus is real, he answers prayers, and is available eight hours a day seven days a week."

Church had stopped meaning anything to her; she spent two years in college studying philosophy and religion. "But found very little of value, in fact it nearly destroyed me. I felt trapped, I had to break out. I took part in sit-ins and riots. I threw bricks and cursed, I took drugs. I was in Washington for one of the 'peace' marches where we stoned and burned cars, and landed in jail. It was all destructive and hopeless. In desperation I had gone to see one of my professors for help, although I knew he was just as mixed up as I was. This man, teaching in a Christian college, didn't believe in anything! He had nothing to offer. I came away empty and lost.

"Then, hitchhiking back to college, I happened to see Love-Inn and stopped. The Lord must have led me there because they took me in. They understood, they loved me without asking questions." Some fifteen people live there, she told us, including the man she was soon to marry. There is a continuous flow of people who are encouraged to leave as soon as they get on their feet. They grow their own food, have their own church, theater, bookstore. They work with Campus Crusade and the Salvation Army, send speakers to high schools and colleges, practice evangelism on the streets.

"We all work, but we all pray, and it's incredible how the Lord provides for our needs. But the real miracles are what happens to people. I have seen the lame walk, the blind see, the drug addict cured. They come in, these kids on drugs, sometimes leading each other. We prayed with one for twenty-four hours and brought him out of it. When he was sane, he accepted the Lord and went off drugs altogether. He'd been on heroin, speed, everything, but he didn't even have withdrawal pains."

She glanced at a dignified couple sitting there, and received their reassuring smiles. "It's as if the Lord has raised up a new church, or many new churches, and the Holy Spirit is reviving people's lives."

The group's rock radio program reaches people who may never have known Jesus, she said. "People driving, people in hospitals or prisons." She read us two letters from a nineteen-year-old whose life had been almost wrecked by drugs and petty crimes. The first was sheer jive talk from jail, mockingly demanding that someone, anyone, prove there was a God or love or anything worth wasting time on earth for. . . . She then read his last letter, written after a long correspondence; a letter full of joy and wholeness, the words of a soul reborn. He was off drugs completely, dedicating his life to helping others: "You have brought light where there was nothing but bitterness and darkness. You gave me a reason for making peace with myself and with the world. You gave me back the God who made me, a God I didn't even believe existed. Now I've got to make up for lost time, I want to show other people that Jesus can do for them what he has done for me."

The girl folded the letter, put it back in her purse.

There was a question-and-answer period, and the first question asked was personal: "What do your parents think of all this?"

Again the girl looked in the direction of the dignified couple. "They had watched me struggling. They knew what I was before and what I am today. They can see the fruits. I think they're glad." She hesitated. "Aren't you, Mother?"

Both heads were high, both parents were smiling, though their eyes were wet. Both of them nodded.

". . . by their fruits ye shall know them. . . ." (How many of us have ever received such a letter?)

Lord, I loved that girl. Thank you for her. As she had made you real to that boy, she made you newly real to me.

Where the Circles Meet

These people, all these people who weave through our lives.

They circle in and out and around and through us. . . . I see them in a long chain, making a figure eight like traffic circles. I am at the point where these circles converge. They have reached me there at the center and driven through me and on . . . and my life remains fixed and yet changed. Changed by their penetration in passing. They have left something of God behind.

How many more there are than the few I have mentioned. Hundreds of others in this endless parade . . . Their faces float before me, their voices linger. . . .

They are your disciples, Lord, walking the roads of the world as it is today. Pounding the hard pavements, ringing doorbells, writing on blackboards, climbing on buses, coping with jobs and children and the trials of everyday. Yet bearing witness to your reality with their words and with their lives.

Thank you that they have cared enough to pause and share your reality with me.

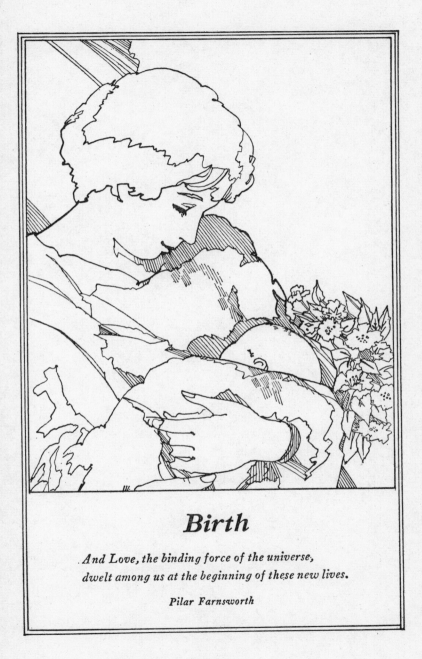

Birth

And Love, the binding force of the universe,
dwelt among us at the beginning of these new lives.

Pilar Farnsworth

I Am!

Birth is surely a direct experience with God.

Any kind of birth . . . A child's birth, yes, that is the highest form of birth for the people who participate or witness it. . . . But the birth of any living thing: Kittens. A colt. Puppies. Out of the warm secret pouch, the safe flesh nest of the mother, into existence of its own. Tiny, blinded by the light, staggered, making noises of protest, the new life comes into the world. Fashioned out of nothing, hurled forth without willing, yet it asserts itself.

"I live, I live, I am!"

Or it breaks out of its egg, its shell, with no less vigor, yelling its right to exist.

That bird, that tiny fallen bird I almost stepped on as a child running home from school . . . It was raw and naked and newly hatched. It was but a scrap of skin and bones attached to a frantic, yawning prong of mouth. But within it blazed and fought the terrible spark of life. It floundered, panted, strained. It was dumb, it could not speak, it made no sound at all, but in a horrible silent scream it begged for its right to *be*.

A friend called, as I remember, and I ran on. (We were always rescuing so many injured creatures, and so many of them died.) But the image of that tiny thing upon the sidewalk has always haunted me. It spoke with such awful eloquence of the mystery of becoming, and our dependence on forces beyond ourselves.

Some of the ancient religions speak of God as the great *I Am*. . . . Yet to each living thing *it* is the great *I Am*. Herein lies the difference: That which is purely created demands attention, its needs must be met. It must be fed, cleansed, attended, taught. . . . God demands nothing; a creator has no such needs. And the cries and demands of his creatures, "I am, I am!" simply demonstrate the power that has brought us out of nowhere into being.

I think it is good for children to watch the birth of pets. It is awesome and heart-stirring. It gives them reverence before the dramatic miracle of life, and the very source of life.

No scientist alive has ever been able satisfactorily to explain to me the how-come of a bug, or a butterfly, or a baby—or me! To be born at all, what a marvel. To emerge out of nothingness, as I've said . . . But no, wait, not entirely *nothing*. There is always a seed, a sperm. Infinitesimal, too small to be seen, yet each holding that essential speck of life.

Of life . . . Ah, therein lies the mystery. For even when we can hold the seed in our hand, as the seed of a flower, or see it beneath a microscope, what secret force lies within it that makes it grow? . . . *Life* . . . And where does life come from and why? What can life possibly be but an act or a fact of an all-powerful Creator?

And growth. How remarkable, growth. "Each thing after its own kind." Multiplication of tissues and cells and the cunning interplay of all the parts . . . Organs that smoothly function, limbs, skin, teeth, and hair . . . Out of what? Nothing, absolutely nothing except its special secret locked in that minuscule seed.

Come on, scientist, mix me up a batch or even a speck of life. Put things in your test tube, the elements, the chemicals. Nucleic acid, for one, which they say contains the basic formula for growth. But wait, we're defeated before we start, because first we must *have* the test tube and the acid; and this is cheating because we have already borrowed from other sources in a world we never made; we are not truly creating at all.

And even if we succeed and life somehow stirs, what will it be? A bird, a beast, a boy? . . . Make me a baby, scientist, with ten fingers and toes and a stomach that hungers and a mouth that cries. Make me a man who can dream. . . . Or make me a flower, a bumblebee, a tree.

I did not always feel this way.

Young and strutting with life, I took life as my due. That precious stuff—where did it *come* from? Are you kidding? From my parents, of course, and their parents before them and on and on back into dim beginnings which failed to bother me. It was all mixed up with biology and genetics and evolution and a lot of things I didn't understand, although I prated of laws of cause and effect and natural selection and everything having a perfectly simple, provable textbook reason because of these natural laws. . . . Not pausing to reason, in my blithe, so-called reasoning, that you can't have laws without a law-giver, or life beyond life beyond life without some ultimate life source.

Then I had a baby. And it taught me a lot about God.

A Child Begins

Out of an emotion a child begins. Out of an impulse, a yearning to be close to another living being, out of an act of love.

What is an act of love but a fusion? Of bodies, yes, but of souls as well. The secret hungering essence of self seeking to find itself and lose itself. Seeking to vanish and begin again. This is true in the most perfect and rapturous sense when the two people deeply love each other. But even when they don't, when on the common, everyday plane they may be miles apart, the mystery of sex can provide an instant out of eternity in which there is genuine union, and out of it a new life can come.

That first child . . . It seemed a tragedy at the time. We were newly married and painfully poor and it seemed an outrage to bring a baby into a world where jobs were scarce and children already went hungry. I fretted and stormed. Yet my body went quietly about its business of fashioning the child within, paying no heed.

It swelled and grew and weighted me down, forcing its will upon me. Making me walk more slowly, move less freely, submit to miseries and indignities. It was in league with something bigger than myself; I, the real me, didn't matter any more. And while a part of me was still protesting and appalled, the rest of me was privately intrigued. . . .

All that threshing and pushing and lunging about, making it hard to rest . . . What was it *doing?* . . . Touch the bulge curiously— here a fist, surely, there a knee—and ask your husband to. Feel the almost comical beating—how a child seems to pound at the doors of its prison, demanding life!

I wanted to laugh sometimes; and—there was no denying it—I was overwhelmed sometimes with the wonder.

No matter how commonplace reproduction, to the mother it is always a signal event. An incredible experience, all these things going on within her, over which she has no control. There is no stopping it, short of abortion. And when the child is ready (never mind about you), it will signal its will to be born.

Whether she acknowledges it or not, a pregnant woman is truly in the grip of God.

At long last it happens. The false alarms are over—you know, you know—and marvel at the quick sure wisdom of your body, cleansing itself, meshing its machinery for the job ahead. . . . Make way, make way, make ready! . . . And you rush about, thrilled, grateful, excited, scared, like a separate thing while the body presses forward on its immutable undertaking. This incredibly strong and knowledge-able body designed so perfectly for its purpose, behaving so splen-didly despite your astonished cries . . .

We were young and far from home, without parents nearby or even neighbors, for we lived in the country, and would the old car start and race us to the hospital in time? And I cried upon God for deliverance, a God I didn't think I knew very well. . . . No mat-ter, something must hold me up, help me, help me, be with me, some strength beyond my strength, some power beyond my power.

I could think of no other name but God's.

Instinctively, blindly, the laboring mother turns to her source. The source of life itself, the life of the child struggling to come forth . . . For at least a few brief moments she dwells with God and is one with God if only because she has been pitched headlong into a pit of elemental suffering.

And nurses gather round to aid and comfort and a doctor in-structs, "Bear down." And you draw gluttonously from the sweet succoring mask, and the blessed cry comes. . . . Your baby cry-ing!

The miracle intact . . . They hold it up for you to see. So tiny and redly squirming . . . life! Raw from the hand of God.

For if ever you have suspected God . . . hoped for God . . . longed to know God . . . grabbed at God for sheer survival . . . or known the bliss of God, it is now.

Though you refuse to phrase it, even with your thoughts, every instinct knows it, every drop of blood. You can never be quite so close to God as in the hour of giving birth.

Thank God for every experience of birth I have had. For every moment of pregnancy and every time of travail. I would not want to

have missed a second of it, Lord. For it tested the body you gave me,
and proved my strength as a woman.

Thank you for this body that can reproduce. A body out of my own
body—what a wonderful thought.

"Be fruitful and multiply" was the command. And this child, these
children, are fruit—fruit of self, yes, but fruit of forces beyond my-
self. I am one with your plan of creation.

And there is a euphoria after birth that must be a foretaste of
heaven. . . . The blissful rest after the fierce struggle. The joy of
holding the hot little body of the new one close . . . Such a delirium
of love comes flooding that it seems too much to hold. It goes beyond
the confines of the child or even the family and longs to embrace all
the people in the world.

And yet for a time the mother and her baby live in a little world
of their own. They have shared some amazing experience, they are
literally heart-close. . . . Why do we automatically hold a new baby
over the left shoulder? I read where one psychologist theorizes it
is probably because it's nearest the heart, whose rhythms soothed
the child as it lay inside the mother so long. Instinctively we rest and
pat him there where he feels most comfortable and safe. . . .

And my love intensified when the baby nursed. To realize he was
drawing sustenance from me added to the vital sense of connection,
making me feel more than ever a part of some profound and thrilling
plan.

But the sense of glory and triumph diminishes, ends. Realities
crowd in. . . . Diapers, night feedings, colic, confusion. Other children and a husband to look after, a house to keep . . . The baby is
a baby no longer and responsibilities multiply on all fronts. The God
who seemed so close during the drama of creation is crowded out,
a dim figure. And you can't simply keep on having birth experiences
to restore him again.

Yet the memory of birth remains. The whole body and being remember. God worked through you and with you; he delivered you
out of the pit and delivered a new life with you.

He loves you. And the next birth can be yours.

Jesus said that to find God each of us must be born again.

Fathers

Men need not miss the experience of birth.

My father stood by my mother's bedside and helped her. Physically helped her, pulling with his hands as was done in those days. Touched her, caressed her, wiped her streaming face, spoke words of loving encouragement to her, suffered with her, and rejoiced with her when their child came. It was he who brought the baby to her to marvel over together. And their love was a deep, eternal thing.

My husband was in the delivery room twice with me, sharing the wonder. He felt denied on the other occasions when he was kept waiting in a hallway or shooed home.

I am glad that natural childbirth is making more men aware of how truly they are partners in this plan of creation. And that there is a strong growing movement to bear children at home. George and Pilar Farnsworth are fervent young leaders in it. Pilar writes: "In our culture we avoid two fundamental moments of life: birth and death. Often birth takes place in a hospital setting under anesthesia—complete flight from experience, total unconsciousness. Other forms of anesthesia let the woman 'see' her delivery: sensation dulled. . . . The moment of birth is a peak, a transcendental, religious experience. People should witness birth and death.

"Our last three children were born at home. An event of the future rather than the past. Professional assistance came to our house. Family and friends were there. And Love, the binding force of the universe, dwelt among us at the beginning of these new lives."

George, her husband, says: "We suggest that a person's ability to achieve sustained love for himself and his fellow men is set and limited by the conditions of his life, and that the moment of birth and the events immediately after play an important role. Birth is the first interaction between a child and the world. It must be an act of love for the mother and everyone else involved."

It is not enough simply to sire a child; men should participate in every possible phase of its beginning, for when they do they come closer to the mother, to the child itself, and whether they realize it or not, to their God.

And so—birth.

Doors open and a visible life appears. The tiny new person made in our image—and in the image of God.

We stand at the very doors of creation. We stand in the presence of God.

Death

A little while, and ye shall not see me:
and again, a little while, and ye shall see me,
because I go to the Father.

John 16:16

And now—death.
Doors close, and a visible life disappears. I no longer
see that image except in memory.
Has he taken God with him? Have I then lost God?

Gone Where?

When someone dies, we say, "He's gone."

It is a hot night in a little Iowa town. . . . Footsteps on the walk
beyond the window, a mysterious knocking at the door . . . My father
rises, I hear the murmur of voices. The door slams, footsteps are
running. . . . I lie heart-pounding, puzzled, filled with foreboding.

At last footsteps return, more slowly. I hear the door open, and my
father's voice in the bedroom, saying, oh so gently to my mother:
"Dear, your father's gone."

"*Gone!*" Her awful cry of disbelief . . . the shock of her moaning.

I lie trying to comprehend it. . . . *Gone* is a difficult word for anyone, let alone a child. . . . To vanish, be no more—inconceivable
. . . *Gone. All gone* . . .

But then a simple resolution presents itself, in the form of a question: "Gone where?" Gone usually meant you went someplace. My
father was a traveling man, gone lots of times on the road. He came
back; he always came home.

And so I remember hopping out of bed and running barefoot to re-
assure her. "Don't worry, he'll be back."

"No, he won't, honey, Grandpa's *gone!*"

"Gone where?"

And she held me and rocked me as she wept, she told me Grandpa
had gone to heaven. But it didn't seem to comfort either of us. . . .
Gone in death meant the trip from which there is no return. I would
never see my adored Grandpa Griffith again, not on this earth, and
I began to whimper, not because I really sorrowed yet, simply because I could not believe it. . . .

Now I realize the validity of that child's question: "Gone where?"
For if we believe the promises of Jesus, we do go somewhere.

We, who are God's dearest creation, cannot simply be stamped out, canceled, obliterated. We are not sticks or leaves to be consumed in the fire, clouds to vanish in the wind; we are so much more than bodies, we are miracles of mind, emotion, spirit! It is this that distinguishes us from all else on the face of the earth, animate or inanimate. We are God's children, his companions, angels (fallen angels, yes, but still his angels).

When one of us leaves the earth, it is for another destination. As surely as if he had climbed on a train that becomes just a plaintive wail in the distance, or a plane that dwindles to a speck in the sky. The rest of us can no longer see the plane or train or bus or car, or its occupant. But we know it is taking him somewhere.

"All aboooard! Let's go!" . . . Whether we are prepared for that summons or not, we all know it's coming—to us and everyone we love. And its very inevitability bespeaks a God firmly in charge. When our time on earth is up (whatever the circumstance, even time foreshortened), God wants us back. He has other plans for us. And no matter how smart we think we are, how independent, how accomplished . . . no matter about our books, speeches, inventions, musical compositions, cures . . . no man or woman is able to say, "Sorry, not me, forget it."

When death says, "Let's go," you *go*.

Good-bys are always hard. Separations always hurt—whether short or long or final. . . . The vacancy, the emptiness, the loneliness, the longing . . . But it helps, how it helps to know that the one we miss so acutely has not ceased to exist, but simply lives in a place where we can't join him yet.

Dad's Roses

Death can be a bridge that leads the living to God as well as it leads those who have left us.

Our love wants to follow, our love refuses to let go.

Our hearts go crying after the dear ones. . . . "Wait for me, wait for me!" . . . But they can't, they must continue on their journey and we know we can't follow, not yet. We can only look up, earthbound.

And yet we sometimes feel their presence so powerfully there is no mistaking it. And with it, the presence of God.

For a long time during the first year after my father died, I was aware of him standing among roses, many roses, on a lovely slope of hill.

He had always loved roses. Those he raised were a source of great pleasure and pride. I can see him yet going out to trim them, wearing a beaten-up old sweat-stained hat that Mother deplored . . . his blunt, work-scarred hands arranging them so gently on the trellis, his ruddy face filled with such pleased affection. Sometimes he'd pause to sniff deeply of their fragrance, then remark to anyone who happened to be near—"Pretty, ain't they?"

Now here he was among the roses, many roses. . . . No, I didn't have a vision, and yet the lovely picture would come to me. He was always smiling faintly, with the familiar twinkle in his eyes, as if there was something delightful he wanted to say. And I knew without question what it must be: "Pretty, ain't they?"

Then he would turn and trudge away.

That was the only sad part of this image. That after it he must go without a backward glance for me.

And yet I did not protest it, for I realized he was in your keeping, God. You had your hand on his shoulder. You would stay close to him and close to me.

This awareness . . . sensation . . . define it as you will, came less frequently after the first hard weeks and ultimately came no more. Yet I remember it vividly and even the memory gives me reassurance. My bright-eyed dad, always so vitally active, had not only gone, he was still going! Though without haste now, without worry or urgency.

He had time to pause and admire the flowers. Time to console me by sharing the wonder. To marvel in his old way—"Pretty, ain't they?"

Mother's Bible

Death can also bridge the estrangements between people.

For twelve years my mother lived on alone in their little house with its roses. . . . Then one day when she was eighty-four . . . one bright day after serving lunch for my two brothers who often popped in for a bite and one of their lively debates on how best to improve the world . . . she hung her apron behind the door and went to join God and Dad.

I wish this were quite as idyllic as it sounds. She had not been feeling well for weeks and I'm sure she sensed that she was going. She had made quite a few little preparations, including leaving instructions, written in her familiar tiny script, in the Bible she always used, on her dresser where we'd be sure to find them.

But one thing uppermost on her mind she had been able to do little about. There had been a feud in the family. One of those agonizing conflicts between grown children that tear a parent apart. She had wept over it, prayed over it, but the wounds were far from healed.

But now that the house was silent and we all came rushing back, everybody forgot. People ran sobbing into each other's arms. And there was so much to be done. There was simply no time for hostilities. . . . Yet they refused to vanish altogether even in the face of death. Though proprieties were maintained, even an extra show of courtesy, after that first surge of emotion you could feel them quivering, threatening.

Then, that second night, we saw her Bible on the coffee table.

Not the "new" one given her on some anniversary years ago to replace the heavy, cumbersome old one with its family records. We had already consulted the "new" one. This was the old one so long ago relegated to the top shelf of the bookcase. Yet here it lay, on a table that had been cleared and dusted several times! Who had gotten it down? . . . Mystified, we consulted each other.

No one else had been here, at least anyone who would have known or cared about that particular Bible. Yet none of us had done so, and each of us was as puzzled as the rest. . . . That Bible simply appeared; there is no other explanation for it.

Without a word everyone sat down while my sister opened the book at its marker. It opened to the thirteenth chapter of John. In a second she began to read aloud:

" 'Now before the feast of the passover, when Jesus knew that his hour was come that he should depart out of this world unto the Father, having loved his own which were in the world, he loved them unto the end.' "

She paused and looked around. All our eyes were wet. Hers went back to the page. "It goes on to tell the story of how Jesus washed the disciples' feet," she said. "And there's this—this place is marked!

'Little children, yet a little while I am with you. Ye shall seek me: and as I said unto the Jews, Whither I go, ye cannot come; so now I say to you. A new commandment I give unto you, That ye love one another; as I have loved you, that ye also love one another.'"

She couldn't go on. She didn't have to. The two who had been so tragically separated groped out for each other's hands. Then they embraced, holding each other as if never to let go.

The peace they made that night was to last. The bridge of death had become the bridge of love that is also God.

Face to Face

I am searching for you, God. I am trying to find you.

Sometimes you are close, as close as my own hand, my own breath. Again you disappear. I get too busy to pray, too busy sometimes even to think.

And though I feel a vague loneliness, unease, it doesn't seem to matter too much. I have all these other people to talk to, warm living people to work for and love and touch.

Then one of them is torn from me. . . . The phone rings. Or an ambulance comes screaming to my steps. . . . A doctor beckons, looking grave. . . .

Then I cry out to you, "My God, my God!" . . . Whether in sheer anguish or anger, I call out to you. Then, as never before, I find you.

Death brings us face to face.

When this happens, all those things I have read or been told—how easy they are to forget. This is not somebody else's concept or philosophy of death. This is *my* death. My flesh-and-blood death to deal with. And now, as at no other time, I must decide whether or not I want any part of God.

But I must realize: If, in my agony, I turn away from God, then I, too, go down into death. The death of all hopes ever to see the one I love again (for I cannot reject God and still claim his promises). And the death of my own spirit. For life can never again have the meaning it had when both he and my God were in it.

If, as I must say good-by to the one who meant so much to me, I also abandon God, then I am doubly bereft.

If, in my pain, my almost intolerable sense of loss, I blame God, I am destroying myself. The words in Job, "Curse God, and die," mean exactly that. To curse God *is* to die in the vital core of self.

Have I ever found God? Do I truly know him? Death puts us to the test. And sometimes the closer we think we have been to God, the more severe the test. . . .

I thought you loved me! I prayed, I had such faith—and now this!

I feel sure God understands. For we are only human, bound to those we care about with such fierce hot human ties. It is natural to weep, protest. (Jesus wept, too, at the death of his friend.) And we are like children; all of us are really children inside these grown-up bodies, especially when we lose someone. Like children we lash out at what we can't understand. Then, when the storm has subsided, we must be comforted. We plunge gratefully into the arms of the person we trust.

This is the time for God. Our own Creator. The one who not only gave us life but created and shared with us the life we loved so much. Where else can we turn for any real assurance that that life or our own lives have any meaning? God alone knows the answers, and in God alone can we find them, through his son.

Living in a time of slavery and slaughter, when life was considered cheap, Jesus told us over and over how precious life is. That not one sparrow falls without God's knowing and caring, not one hair of our head is harmed . . . Living in a hot and arid country, where only the winter rains fill the cisterns or there is a single well for the town, he knew how constantly people were thirsty. Yet he spoke of the deeper thirst, the thirst for God. He told us to drink of the well of living waters, that we might have life everlasting. He told us that our time here is but the flick of an eye compared to eternity, and actually only preparation for the richer life beyond.

We hear those words so often at funeral sermons we forget they were not preached as funeral sermons. Jesus was speaking to people in farms and shops and homes, on busy highways and village streets. Not in hushed chapels with organ music playing and the heavy fragrance of floral wreaths. Not simply to comfort the bereaved. What he was telling those people, and us, was meant as a challenge to a more abundant, generous, God-trusting life here that would lead to an even greater life.

He had come to spread the good news. He had come to show us how. And he was going ahead to be sure that all was ready for us.

There is comfort in those words, yes. But I must forget I have heard them at funerals (the heart can break at funerals). I must go to my Bible and read them for myself. There they have a different sound, crisp, fresh, sure, inviolate. Their truth sings out, flinging wide the doors that seem to mark the close of life.

I can look beyond them, and see the wonders beyond those doors.

I have found you, God, I have found you.
Death has brought us face to face.
I know you, I trust you, I believe in your promises.
I claim them for the one who has gone on before me, and I claim them for myself.

Promises to Keep

"The Lord gave, and the Lord hath taken away. . . ."

That familiar quote from Job. Mr. Malone used to challenge this. (The minister in our little Christian church at home.) Got almost angry when he heard people speak of God's "taking" someone. "The Lord didn't take that child," he said. "A germ did." "The Lord didn't strike that man. A car did."

We are all subject to natural laws. When something goes wrong, when a law is broken, disaster follows. . . . But God is the author of the universe, source of those natural laws. Can't he change things to please us? What about miracles? What about prayers?

It is all such a mystery; we study and speak and search and discuss and know so little. Erudite as we try to sound, we know, actually know so little.

That's got to be where faith comes in. . . . Do we ever need faith quite so much as when a life is snapped off unexpectedly? Suddenly, shockingly, one day here, the next day gone. A young life, especially, so full of joy and promise . . . Faith, no matter what. The deep wordless recognition that what *is* must be accepted and does not mean God has abandoned us, nor intentionally done that young life in. . . . But God's *will?* No, I don't think we'd better get faith fouled up with God's will. . . .

That little girl rushing home from school eager to show her mother her drawing and a report card full of A's . . . How can I believe in a God who would decide: "Aha, I shall cheat that mother of even that brief happiness, I won't even let her reach the doorstep, I'll take that child right now!"

Or my friends Frank and Sara Foster, en route to a Baptist convention with another ministerial couple, Joe and Diane Wortman. Beautiful parents with two children apiece; both had built flourishing churches; they'd witnessed in the streets and were planning a camp for homeless boys. . . . So much accomplished already, so rich a harvest ahead . . . "The convention is waiting for them; Sara is supposed to sing (I gave her the voice of an angel). Nobody doubts they'll get there, but I've got other plans for them. I'll send a storm to bring that small plane down. . . ."

No, I don't even want to find a God like that. Any god worthy of my worship at least has common sense. And my God is a god of mercy, of fair play and compassion as well as a god of power (who can and continually does work miracles and answer prayers). My God would never deliberately bring harm to anyone. But if it happens—if it simply happens due to wind and rain and weather and man's own mistakes, then God has promises to keep:

Life continuing. An even richer, fuller, brighter ongoing life to compensate.

Lord, dear Lord, I will hold fast to you and remember:

You did not take those young lives, but you received them. (How gently and how generously you received them!)

You did not will their going, but you accept their return.

You did not cut short their time of growth and happiness on earth, but you will enhance and enrich their time of growth and happiness where they have gone.

I will not grieve for what they have lost, I will rejoice for what they have gained.

I will not blame you for what happened; but I will thank you for what is happening now. To them, as they know you in person. To me, as I know you in spirit.

Thank you that your love can turn tragedy into triumph.

So Short, but Oh So Sweet

And I must remember this about the death of the young. Sometimes a mission on earth can be accomplished in a very few years. (Jesus didn't live very long either.) Isn't it possible that the work someone may have been sent to do is finished?

Not in the case of those young ministers. No, no, that seems senseless; they were all set to help so many more, to do so much more *good*. But others? At least some others?

One thing is certain: A short life can be an intensely sweet one; almost always sweeter and purer than a life prolonged. Any parent who has lost a child acknowledges this. You sorrow for the joys of life that child has missed, but you recognize the pain and problems it has been spared. It goes back to its maker unembittered, unscarred, leaving only the most beautiful memories behind.

And we know—every instinct knows with some deep knowledge—that life does not stop, whatever its stage of interruption; it continues to develop in perfection. And usually far happier than it could possibly be in this precious but battle-wracked existence.

Quite a body of evidence is accumulating about the life experience beyond. Repeatedly, people who have been close to death, or who have actually died according to medical tests, who remember actually crossing over before being brought back by modern scientific technics, such people insist they experienced such joy, such unimaginable peace and transport that they didn't want to return.

The Procession

The more people I lose to death, the nearer to God I am. I had not realized this until recently, and yet it's true.

When I was young, death was a terrifying stranger who snatched one of my playmates one night. I wept wildly and strove to join him by climbing as high as I dared in the maple tree.

Later, impossibly, the town lifeguard and hero drowned, and we were all in a state of shock; but it was mass emotion and unreal. Our grandparents died, but that was the way of the old. Our parents frequently mourned for friends and relatives and went to funerals, but what had that to do with us, the young? For we were, of course, immortal. . . . And yet, in the haunted catacombs of our souls he lurked, that threatening stranger. "No, no, he dare not touch us, we were too young, we hadn't lived yet, and besides we would live forever!"

Then Tommy crashed. My aviator cousin with his grand helmet and goggles, who was going to teach me to fly. And I knew then it wasn't the old and tired and life-used that death relished and stalked, it was the young. And I was horrified and frightened. It was all wrong and cruel, it had nothing to do with God.

But death becomes less of a stranger as we grow older. No less cruel when we have to give up someone we love. But a force we can accept. Now we are the ones attending the funerals while our immortal young run free. We have learned how to say good-by to people, so many people, and go on from where we were. (Sometimes straight from their services to a party.) Besides, death has been all doctored up now, as if you're not supposed to notice. People don't carry on the way they used to, at least where they can be seen; sometimes they don't even have funerals. It's more as if the one who's died has just moved away.

Yet if you care . . . if you truly care.

The pain that seems at times beyond bearing. The aching vacancy that begs somehow to be filled. Speak of him, oh speak of him— reminisce about him with others, talk about the good times, laugh so you won't cry. . . . And this is good for a while; it helps to be with people who knew him, who can share the memories. But watch out lest you try to make their company a substitute for the one who can't return. No other living person and no amount of talk can re-create him for you. So let go of them, let go as quickly as you can.

And the letters, the pictures, the garments hanging mute in the closet. The records you listened to together, the little jokes and souvenirs. What of these? What of these? . . . Let go. Gradually, little by little, let go; for we must stop reaching backward toward the places our dear ones have left before we can reach out and upward toward the place where they *are*. Stop hugging them to your breast in grief. Open your arms to embrace them in prayer.

Back in those days when I was so young I remember a minister's saying we ought to pray for the departed. I couldn't imagine why. They'd lived and died, for them it was all over, I thought, their fate was sealed. How could they possibly need or want my prayers?

But when you are older and have lost someone, you don't have to ask. You find youself praying, not so much for them as for yourself, because it seems the only way to make contact. . . . "Oh, Cindy—" . . . "Oh, Mother—" . . . "Oh, John—" . . .

Dear God, let them know I love them and am thinking of them. Please take care of my darlings.

And gradually the tone of the prayer changes—at least it did for me. I found it became less a cry of desperate longing than a prayer of loving release. A message of blessing. A time to remember those I loved and to rejoice that they were safely in God's gardens. Like my dad.

You get used to anything, even intense personal loss. And you get used to the more and more frequent departures. This relative. That. A close friend. Another friend. A neighbor, a beloved teacher, your boss . . . You even get used to receiving that first shock. *No. I can't believe it—not him!* . . . There seems no rhyme or reason so often, no special order, only that there are always more. And more.

Until after a while it dawns on you how many there are. It must be getting crowded in heaven! When you try to remember them in prayer, you have to call the roll. But there is something actually joyful in the thought. . . . They are not alone up there. They have "the blessed company of heaven."

And quietly, steadily, all unseen, this procession of departures has been leading you closer to God.

At least so it was with me. With every one who leaves, I am being drawn, without knowing it, just a little nearer to the original source who designed their destination. And my own.

For as surely as he sent me to this earth, he has given me a return ticket. I know that one day I, too, will be in that same procession. I will join them. . . . And the mere fact that I call their names in prayer, lifting them up, asking for them peace and joy and all of God's blessings, confirms the fact that they are *there*. As I, too, will one day be there.

And so I don't fear death any more, or doubt God any more.

Death has helped me to find him.

Reading

*Whosoever shall read this writing, and shew
me the interpretation thereof, shall be clothed
with scarlet, and have a chain of gold about his neck.*

Daniel 5:7

The Sorcerer's Apprentice

I am trying to find God.

I say that I want to know him better—and yet I neglect him. It is like a friendship that dies for lack of attention; a correspondence that ultimately stops because one of us won't write. If I am to maintain my relationship with God, I have to read his letters. And I must also read the letters of people he has inspired to tell of their own search and discovery. If I am too lazy or indifferent, it's like turning away hungry from a table groaning with food.

"I'm starved," the spirit cries. "Help me, feed me or I will die." Yet when someone says, "Here, eat," I must be willing to pick up the spoon.

And so—books. And a heady abundance of other publications. What an avalanche of words; how they fill the mails and the house. Like *The Sorcerer's Apprentice*. I have asked for nourishment, and I almost have to open the doors for the rich porridge that overflows. Praise God for it. It helps to counteract the tide of violence and obscenity that pours from the presses. I simply protest my inability to explore but a fragment of it. For I have never picked up a magazine, tract or leaflet having to do with God that I did not receive a ray of enlightenment and a sense of his presence.

And so instead of crying, "Stop, stop!" as the apprentice did to the sorcerer, I should be thankful and somehow make room. Store them against the hour when I can at least sample them. For, I repeat, never have I done so without receiving a blessing. People throughout the world are writing things that can help us. Famous people sometimes, but more often a preacher or missionary just doing his job with zeal; a housewife, a laborer sharing their experiences in prayer and faith and healing. Or often revelations that surely come from the infinite mind to which, if we are listening, we are all attuned.

"Where do ideas come from?" a child asked me. "How does anybody know anything for sure?" And then before I could answer: "I guess God just tells him."

He was right. Often when we can't figure things out for ourselves, or the usual paths to wisdom are too long and arduous or faulty, God says: "Here, it's like this." He just tells us. . . . And remarkably, he often tells a lot of widely scattered people the same thing at the same time. When this happens, there are often break-throughs in formal spheres of knowledge; and there are constant daily break-throughs in average minds. Every now and then we discover, seemingly out of nowhere, truths to which we must witness in words. Written words . . .

Thus the magazines, booklets, newspaper clippings. Many of mine old and yellow, worn and marked. . . . Once, moving, and about to throw out an unread accumulation, I came upon one that provided a clear ringing answer to a question that had bothered me for years.

Help me never to turn my back on such things, Lord, nuisance that they sometimes seem. They are not a nuisance—they are manna from heaven sent to fill a need.

Books That Have Helped Me

I hold a book in my hand. A much used book, the binding frayed, many of its passages underscored. I have never met the author and never will, for his typewriter has been stilled for years. Yet I feel I have always known him and he has known me, for he wrote this particular book for me.

And he wrote it for you, God. Through you. So I do know the author in a way, because he was sharing with me the thoughts you gave him, he was laboring to set down the words you willed.

And as he was and is a part of you, he made me realize how much I, too, am a part of you.

I gaze at my cluttered shelves. Books stacked atop each other, spilling onto the floor. Some as familiar as this dear one in my hand, some brightly jacketed and new. I am both happy and sad at sight of them, for I know—as with the articles—I can't do justice to them. Many of these books, so full of love and knowledge, are like old and treasured friends who urge, "Call us, come to see us." While there is the tantalizing promise of the new. Yet the days are so full. I have so little time to seek out the friends who mean the most to me, let alone enjoy my new ones. But how wonderful to know I can always go to them.

Mr. Walleck, an old bookseller in Pittsburgh, once told me: "A man who had a library of ten thousand books and seldom read a one would still be a better man. Books have a life quality of their own. They are a condensation of mental energy. The man, even though he didn't recognize it, would still be supported by the fact that he could go to them at any time and visit with the greatest minds of the ages."

Thank you for these books, Lord, read and unread.

The ones that have touched me lightly, and those that have etched so deeply. Those that have already taught me so much, and those from which I still have so much to learn.

Help me to hang on to their truths. Guide me again to the truths that await me in their pages.

The Book About Healing

Healing, Lord, what can books teach me about healing?

For I need healing. . . . My soul in its search needs healing. My body sometimes becomes so weary it seems it can't go on. My mind is heavy with its weight of worry. My soul longs to be released and run free.

Most of Jesus' miracles had to do with healing. The disciples healed, too, and were told to pass their healing powers on. . . . Lord, if I am to believe in you and walk close to you, I must believe in your power to heal today.

I must know more about healing.

I know that healing is a mystery as well as a science. Even doctors don't know why or how it happens, only that sickness and injury of body or mind sometimes yields to medical treatment and sometimes doesn't. How strange. Despite inoculations to prevent many dread diseases and miracle drugs to overpower infections . . . despite marvelous advances in surgical technics (kidney and heart transplants, surgical cunning that is awesome) . . . despite new (or sometimes very old) knowledge about healing powers from the earth itself—vitamins, minerals, herbs, and the revival of the ancient art of acupuncture . . . despite all this, there is still so much we long to know about healing.

What about spiritual healing? Healing that goes beyond science or seeming reason; the kind Jesus performed with a touch or sometimes a look. Healing that surpasses even the medical miracles and often must accompany them if they are to succeed. Healing that continued to be performed by his followers after he was gone; that was, in fact, a vital function of the early church. Repeatedly the disciples did what they were told to—and found they could! "There came also a multitude out of the cities round about unto Jerusalem, bringing sick folks, and them which were vexed with unclean spirits; and they were healed every one" (Acts 5:16).

What a pity this serious responsibility was allowed to slip away as scientific discoveries were made, so that ultimately it was ignored by all but a few cults. (Though we prayed for the sick when I was a child, nobody even considered the Lord's promises and commands about healing. That even the most devout could be a channel for *healing?* Don't be silly.) Yet now, strangely, when medical miracles boggle the mind, we see an astonishing return to healing, spiritual healing.

Faith healers on radio and TV. Healing services in the most conventional churches, accompanied by anointing and laying on of hands. Prayer groups working together for specific individuals to be healed . . .

Is this mass hysteria? A symptom of the epidemic soul sickness ravishing our world? (Wars, riots, kidnappings, senseless murders. Child abuse, mass rapes. Drugs and runaway children. Foul language and fouler pornography. Alcoholism, sexual license, VD. Suicides, overdoses.) For every gain made over disease, for every new medication or machine for curing the body, new and more horrible attacks have come from all directions to destroy both body and soul. In our desperation we know we've *got* to find some help beyond man's fine but tragically unequal efforts.

And that, God, leads us straight to you. When all else fails, we've got to turn to you. If you have the power to create us, you have the power to heal us.

I want to know more about that power.

God's Healing Power. By Edgar L. Sanford. The book that spoke to me when I was badly in need of restoration.

It had been sent to us by my husband's sister Margaret, with a lot of other religious and inspirational books she was always showering on us. Spiritually—and spirited!—she would urge, "Now read this, it'll do you a lot of good." But we were so blithely indifferent; too busy, we thought. The books accumulated, lovingly inscribed, seldom read. . . . Poor Margaret. We used to feel guilty—she meant so well.

Then one day long after its title had stopped accusing me from the shelf . . . one day when someone very dear to me was wracked with pain and my own cup was bitter . . . I was propelled to that bookshelf, blindly seeking comfort, any kind of comfort, and reached for the first book at hand. And it was *God's Healing Power.* (Published by Prentice-Hall, 1959.)

So maybe that's why that book surpasses all the works about healing I have read since. (And there are many. "Seek and ye shall find.") It was a book that made me understand this marvel as I had never done, and it set up forces that resulted, I am convinced, in a chain of personal healing affecting not only those close to me, but the secret, deeper agonies of myself.

It became *my* book of healing.

The author was a minister who discovered early in his career that God's healing power is available to *everybody,* not merely the spiritually gifted. He was instrumental in countless healings both here and in China, where he was for years a missionary. Primarily by teaching people how to claim that power to heal themselves.

I used to hesitate about spiritual healing . . . except as something that I practiced privately. I feared disillusionment . . . in the case of those who might not get well. I soon got over that. The many remarkable recoveries . . . were too important to be ignored. Moreover, there were the grateful testimonials to a deeper sense of God's companionship and love that people expressed when they did know and participate in the therapy.

As one woman wrote him: "Though I have not found bodily health, I have found something else much more important. I have found my God whom I had lost for so long."

The book is filled with exciting miracles of healing. But its true excitement lies in its premise—that all life be approached as a spiritual adventure. It made me aware that I, too, could "work out a program for my soul to follow that will be all the better because it is my very own, one that I have worked out myself, with God."

The Book About Prayer

Books about prayer . . . All the articles and booklets and books, bound and paperback, about prayer . . . So many people knew how to pray long before I did, and how they tried to teach me, how willing they were to share. And, floundering—now believing, now disbelieving, most of the time too busy for them (I thought), but sometimes out of curiosity, sometimes driven by sheer desperation, I reached for what they had to say.

Some I found too pious, some too analytical, some just plain boring. (Were they? Probably not for others, only for me at the time. The soil of my soul was too hard; it needed tilling and even the enriching of real trouble before it was ready to receive.) Occasionally one would strike me: Aha, the magic formula! Say it, rub the bottle (no, make it the Bible), and out would pop the genii (no, make it an angel) to resolve all my problems, hand me whatever I asked for.

And I tried the formulas. How vainly, foolishly, insistently I tried them—and how mad I got when they didn't work. My children didn't get to be prom queen, my husband didn't land the big contract, the story I was writing for *Ladies' Home Journal* bounced back more swiftly than before.

Now and then, yes maybe, a taste of joy, a whiff of relief . . . a sense of something more . . . Only I wasn't asking for the right things for the right reasons, and so I blamed the books. Skip it, forget it, take away your books on prayer. . . . Dear God, if there is a God, I will blunder my own sloppy way to you in my own sloppy method of so-called prayer.

Then one day a favorite friend and editor lent me a small book by Stella Terrill Mann, *Change Your Life Through Prayer*. It, too, had been published years before (1945 by Dodd, Mead). I loved this editor, admired her intelligence. . . . Okay, to please her (and heaven knows my life needed changing). So I opened the book and the first lines of the preface said:

Dear Reader: This book has come to you. Since nothing can come to you except that which belongs to you or that which you need for your growth, accept it as an answer to a need, and do not let the book go until it gives you a blessing. . . .

Me? This book had been written for *me*? And it was to bring me a blessing? . . . I turn the page, and as I read on something begins to happen. Phrases spring up and come running to meet me, like friends the heart has always known but never before recognized:

> *What* do you want?
> What do *you* want?
> What do you *want?*

And:

> Take it as absolute truth that every thought creates after its kind. The only law of supply is the law of abundance, just as the only law of light and energy is the incessant radiation of the sun. . . .

And: *Pray in the Morning . . . Pray While You Work . . . Pray While You Rest.* . . . And singing over and over through all, repeatedly the word "blessing." Bless every circumstance of your life, good or bad, bless every person with whom you come in contact, bless every act. . . .

My blood beats a little faster, love surges from me toward this woman whose life, as she relates it, is very like my own. I can identify with her examples. And the things she is telling me are things I already know, but simply didn't recognize before. And some of the things she recommends I am, praise God, already doing, albeit without being aware of it.

I realize, rejoicing, that I am not a hopeless castaway, but safely aboard; on the right ship even if I have been sailing erratically in the dark without much sense of direction. Now suddenly she turns on the floodlights, adjusts my compass, and says, "Hi, isn't this a great trip? And we're heading for a great landing." Something like that . . . Anyway I am thrilled, released, in a sense reborn.

I want to kick up my heels and excitedly re-explore areas I already know so well: My kitchen, my study, my own back yard. My husband, my children, my friends. How beautiful, how blessed, for all the work and sometimes misery they cause . . . I was already proclaiming their beauty and wonder in most of my writings—magazine articles and newspaper columns—for I am a born life-lover, no matter what. Even at the risk of seeming a hypocrite I have written of love and laughter sometimes out of the very pit. (For by now the dry cracked soul had been deeply plowed by pain and generously watered with tears.)

Now I was ready to receive. And it was if, as I read that little book, I began to see *why* I had been able to write that way. Because God had never really left me for a minute. Even though my mind wouldn't admit it, my heart knew. And God is love and God is good.

Now the next step: Consciously to relate all this to its true source. To thank God and praise him and take inventory of all the blessings I had. Then to see how they could be used, through the power of God, to improve any life situation and lead to better things. When I did this, writings that might have been sheer whistling in the dark became genuine singing in the light!

And I tried the secret of blessing. To bless every person who crossed my path, every circumstance, every encounter, every moment of my life. It has become a habit, and the abundance of blessings pours back.

You have inspired many people, God, and sent them to show others the way. Thank you that I can go back now to books I once rejected and gain from them. And thank you for the new books that enlarge and deepen my love for you. But thank you especially for this book that came to me when I needed it and was ready to receive. A book that became a part of my life and as its title promised: changed my life through prayer.

The Book That Gave Me God Back

Is there total order back of all our seemingly disorderly lives? "A divinity that shapes our ends, rough-hew them how we will," as my mother used to quote? Frankly, I don't know. I just know it is often the "accidents" that do more to affect our lives than the planned events.

A dreary day during my long period of agnosticism and skepticism . . . "Antiquing." (Prowling through jumbled junk shops seeking furniture to be salvaged and glassware for a window shelf.) And being drawn, as usual, to the cases of books . . . Fingering, tasting, getting lost. And sometimes, when an impatient companion calls, just grabbing several because they are so cheap.

Ten cents. Crayoned in the corner of *The Reality of the Religious Life,* by Henry Bett, an English author I'd never heard of. Published by Macmillan way back in 1949. I hadn't the faintest intention of ever reading it—the very title put me off, but it was a first edition, for ten cents. . . .

What made me pick it up again one bright spring day while cleaning house? What caused me to sit on the floor, surrounded by those piles of other read and unread books, and open it to skim the brief introduction? Why was I grabbed by the concluding words of that introduction:

> *There is absolutely no real reason whatever,* in science or philosophy or any other realm of human knowledge, why we should not believe that God guides our lives, and that He answers our prayers, in very strange, unforeseen and unforeseeable ways. . . .

Skeptical but intrigued, I proceeded to Chapter 1: "The Possible and the Credible." Okay, okay, show me. . . . And the morning vanished, suddenly it was time to whip through lunch, and I read the rest of the day away and into the night, and before I had finished Chapter 3, "Causation," walls had come crumbling down—some with a bang, most with a whimper, *because I wasn't really sure I wanted to believe in you, God, for all my on-again, off-again seeking.*

But here was a logical mind at work proving for me the formerly impossible. . . . No scriptural quotations, no talk about salvation, no theology or doctrinology or exhortation or anything else except a brilliant intellect patiently, stubbornly, calmly following unswerving lines to logical conclusions. A man who didn't bury his arguments in verbiage yet didn't talk down to me either. Who, in simple, straightforward language, made it impossible for me ever again to doubt a Creator who brought the universe into being and would be forever in charge of it. Like it or not!

I found such statements as:

No one denies the existence of order in the actual working of the universe from moment to moment. Every scientist . . . takes it for granted that events are actually related to one another, and do actually depend upon one another, in a regular sequence of causation, and to that extent there is a universal order. But is that order purposive or merely automatic? Our belief as to that depends upon our conception of the origin of existence. What was it that at the beginning established what everyone must admit is the subsequent orderliness of the universe? . . .

The materialist rules out intelligence and purpose and direction at the beginning, and then says, in effect, that all that happens is determined by the nature of primal matter at the beginning of the universe. That means (if indeed it means anything) that all the infinitely complex interactions of all the forces and laws of the universe for millions of years were ordered from a beginning when there was no order and no source from which order could come. . . . It is like saying that a mass of jumbled type on the floor of a printer's shop sorts itself out, sets itself up, and prints itself into a sensible book. It is really even madder than that, for the type has at any rate been designed by intelligence. . . . The universe in its actual being from age to age is a realm of causes, laws and order. . . . But the whole of it all, we are told, was a causeless, lawless, orderless chaos of matter, which nevertheless was the matrix of universal destiny. One would think that a really sceptical mind would find it considerably easier to accept the wildest legends of the Middle Ages than to believe in such a cosmogony as that.

And:

The only rational answer . . . is that all the order of the universe is from a Universal Mind which designed it before the beginning, and which directs and effectuates all things continually.

This book clarified so many things for me. Gave me an astounded new understanding . . . About the miracles of Christ. About evil and will and suffering. Yet it is so unevangelical in tone, so almost prosaically believable that it left me stripped of all my objections, challenges, defenses. Emotionally I was almost as staggered as I had been when, as a college freshman, that professor so ruthlessly stripped me of God.

I still had a long way to go and much to learn to make up for lost time. I still had (and will always have) spiritual problems to resolve. Yet this book reached me at a time when, though I didn't suspect it, I was ready to believe.

I try to remember this when I question why you didn't lead me to it long before. . . . For everything there is a time and a season. . . . I probably would have resisted, shrugged, tossed it aside, or thrown up blocks that kept me from comprehending.

No, back of everything is a cause is a cause is a cause, all in a complex yet logical web of wisdom that I recognize finally as the hand of my personal God.

Anyway, never again would I feel apologetic or ignorant or superstitious about believing. Never again need I be intimidated or even impressed by the so-called erudition of anyone—scholar, philosopher, or scientist—who insisted on a material explanation for everything and attempted to prove the universe and life itself a mindless, purposeless accident. Such people might be able to outargue me (as I had outargued my poor mother) but they could never convince me. That book had given me back God.

A Banquet

Other books have helped me. So many others . . . I must tell of at least a few.

There are the books of that true child of God, Catherine Marshall. It was my privilege to become her friend through a little writing group when we first moved to Washington, D.C. Peter Marshall was already gone. Her book *A Man Called Peter* and the movie from it had drawn people to God and to her from around the world. She was then working on *To Live Again* and thereafter *Beyond Our-selves*. It was she who looked at me sometimes with a kind of calm, patient, contemplative understanding. A gaze that I could not meet. (Was this the way the Lord looked at some of those who longed to follow him, but were afraid?)

But later, when my own life had been taken apart and was being tremulously reassembled, I was ready for what the books of Catherine Marshall had to say. *Beyond Ourselves* particularly. This book is so full of help for the troubled spirit, so bursting with the reality of a power beyond our own that I shan't attempt to describe its contents. I can only urge others to read it. And now her latest, *Something More,* which surpasses even that in its clear vision of a constant, ever-caring Creator.

Oh, the rich banquet of books . . .

The works of Emmet Fox, especially *The Sermon on the Mount* and *The Lord's Prayer.* Such lean spare prose, such a mental laser beam illuminating deeper meanings . . . And everything Harry Emerson Fosdick wrote . . . And *The Healing of Sorrow,* by Norman Vincent Peale. To me, one of the most convincing works ever written about the reality of the hereafter.

God-centered works can be as gripping as good fiction. . . . Roy Wilkins' *The Cross and the Switchblade.* How a country preacher was led to go blundering into the toughest ghettos of New York, and through sheer gutty love and faith brought whole gangs of lost, murderous kids to the Lord . . . And *Turned On to Jesus,* by Arthur Blessitt, who worked the same miracles with drug-addicted runaways on Hollywood Strip. And when the conventional establishment tried to destroy His Place, where they found refuge, he chained himself to a cross, fasting and praying until they relented.

Lord, Lord, could I do as much for you if put to the test?
Would I be able to endure what today's martyrs are still enduring behind the Iron Curtain? Tortured for their faith, brutally tortured . . . I'm afraid I wouldn't bear up long.

I didn't think I could even *read* about torture until *In God's Underground* came into my hands. But I had to, something drove me into it, past the jacket that told me its author, Richard Wurmbrand, a converted Jew, had spent fourteen years in Rumanian prisons because he would not collaborate with the conquering Communists. And there, starved, beaten, savagely tortured, his faith actually grew. He determined to use suffering as an opportunity to win souls for Christ—and did! . . .

Others . . . They stand out like vivid landmarks along my journey.

A little "Devotional Diary" called *God Calling* sent me by a woman I'd never met. Written by two British women who say it was dictated by the Holy Spirit and they take no credit for it. Open it to any page and the answer to any question, any problem, appears as if straight from God. . . . Ah, those British. Another little book, *Daily Light,* a compendium of Scriptures to be read morning and night. "Take, eat," said the English friend who gave it to me. "It will be bread for the spirit when you wake and nourish you until you return to it tired at bedtime, to put yourself into his hands even while you rest."

And Albert Schweitzer's *Out of My Life and Thought* . . . And Leo Tolstoi's *The Kingdom of Heaven Is Within You,* with its beautiful introduction by Mary Martin. (What a crazy mixed-up man, Tolstoi, what a savage struggling to be a saint. Yet his very struggles jolted me into awareness.)

And then Brother Lawrence . . . Dear Brother Lawrence—what kindred spirits we must have been for hundreds of years, though I had never heard of him until my own book, *I've Got to Talk to Somebody, God,* appeared, and somebody said: "Like Brother Lawrence, scouring his pots in a monastery kitchen and thanking God for the task." . . . And feeling embarrassed at my ignorance, I found the wafer-thin book setting down his conversations in 1666. And he said . . . he said . . . but how to choose from the pristine gold of *he saids?* . . .

That we need only to recognize God intimately present with us, to address ourselves to him every moment . . .

That his prayer was nothing else but a sense of the presence of God . . . so that he passed his life in continual joy . . .

That we ought not to be weary of doing little things for the love of God, who regards not the greatness of the work, but the love with which it is performed . . .

He found that books only puzzled and discouraged him, so he evolved his own methods:

> I make it my business only to persevere in his Holy presence . . . an habitual, silent and secret conversation of the soul with God . . .

> There is not in the world a kind of life more sweet and delightful than that of a continual conversation with God. . . .

All this while he scrubbed floors and kettles and emptied garbage! . . . The most menial tasks glorified and blessed by the presence of God.

Again a shout of recognition roused up in me. I was on the right ship again and this time sailing unconsciously in the right direction. But the glimmers of joy I had long felt, the wholehearted gratefulness for life and the source of life, could be enhanced and multiplied by taking the advice of this little monk who graced the earth so long before me: *consciously* practicing the very presence of God.

How? Never mind how, just do it! And because I willed it so, it began to happen. The daily dialogues, mental or oral, began to take on a new dimension whenever I thought: *The presence of God. I am in the very presence of God.* Something happens. A joy, a pervading radiance, "an inward emotion so charming and delicious," as Brother Lawrence phrased it, it is almost foolish to try to describe.

You move into me, Lord. You build the very Kingdom of Heaven within me. I sense your shining presence in and all about me— wherever I am, whatever I'm doing. . . . Making a bed, waiting at the check-out counter, driving a car—no matter, no matter, your brilliance possesses me. I want to smile at people, to call out blessings, to sing, to dance.

No, this ecstasy can't last. But then I have other responsibilities that a simple monk with only his God and his simple tasks did not. I turn back to the cashier, the telephone, the countless distractions . . . yet the glow remains. And I am reassured by knowing that just below the surface it lies, ready to be reclaimed. Ready to spring up at a word, a wish—the very presence of God.

A word of warning. Brother Lawrence found that books only confused him. And all people don't respond to the same books. One that
inspired Catherine Marshall, Hannah Whitall Smith's *A Christian's
Secret of a Happy Life,* somehow failed to touch me. Despite the
enthusiasm of many people, I'm afraid I will never be able to wade
through *The Confessions* of St. Augustine or the *Summa Theolog-
ica* of St. Thomas Aquinas. I leave them to the scholars, they are not
for me.

So some of my favorites may not be for you. No matter, there are
plenty of others just waiting to help you. If you, too, are on a diligent
search for a more real God, you will find them. They were written
for you—a hundred years ago perhaps, or as recent as yesterday.
God and truth are ageless. And all writers draw consciously or unconsciously upon the past.

The Bible

And so, as I try to find God I read all these books written by people. God has given them words—to help me ask my questions, to
help provide the answers. Yet even before any of them sat down
at their desks this morning—or a thousand years ago—God had
provided a book of his own. The Bible. Also known as the Word,
because for generations countless multitudes of people have accepted
it as *his word:* God's own communication with us, dealing in un-
changing principles, telling us things no other source can give us con-
cerning him and our relationship to him. Thus if I really want to
know God and what he wants for me, I must go to the source.

"In the beginning was the Word, and the Word was with God, and
the Word was God." The first word. And in modern parlance "the
last word." Because it was given by the creator of all the writers and
the original author of all their words. So let all the rest of us shut up,
"keep silence before him," and all our books be destroyed, his word,
the Bible, would survive. Why? Because he said so, and he *is* the
final word.

Now for years I quarreled with the Bible. The Old Testament
particularly. Impatient, brandishing that "little learning [which] is
a dangerous thing," primed to be cynical, it was all too easy to
pounce on contradictions and preposterous-seeming events (the story
of Balaam's ass, for instance); too convenient to be shocked at the

behavior of some of its protagonists. (And my skepticism was enhanced by the literalists who insisted every word had been personally dictated by God, hence the whole book was infallible and
free of error.) I had totally failed to recognize, let alone grasp, the
over-all purpose back of God's method of revealing himself. A purpose clarified in Louis Cassels' *Your Bible:*

> The Old Testament shows how God made himself known, gradually
> and patiently over many centuries, by entering into an intensely
> personal and often stormy relationship with a particular group of
> people, the Jews, whom he had chosen to be light-bearers to
> mankind. The prophets and kings and other leaders through whom
> God spoke remained very human and very fallible. Even the best
> of them—like the great King David—were guilty of sordid and
> selfish acts, which are plainly recorded in the Bible, as though to
> drive home the point that no matter how open they may have
> been to God's guidance they remained weak and imperfect human
> beings.

The New Testament I could relate to, love. Thrilled if mystified
by its basic premise: that "God emptied Himself of His transcendental majesty and took on the limitations of humanity in the person of
Jesus Christ." True, the Trinity threw me for a long time, but even
that confusion dwindled before the beauty and wonder of Jesus. . . .
And in the years since, during the long search since, as Jesus has
become more real to me, the more vital and rewarding it has been
to explore the Old Testament again. See it with new eyes. With
his eyes.

For if I pray for guidance and understanding, I receive it. It is
like a blind man being led to the table, then suddenly given sight. I
see, I see, I can partake! Not clumsily, gropingly, unsurely as before.
But choosing freely from this generous banquet, savoring, digesting,
comprehending its true beauty and value, knowing at last its power
to nourish me.

Meanwhile, it helps to have a few really good scholars looking
over your shoulder. Historians and linguists and others who have
made a life study of this fascinating book. The Lord inspired not only
the earthly authors of his story, he has inspired and equipped people
who can give us insight today. For me the Jerusalem Bible has been

an invaluable aid. All the background information is right *there*. In introductions to every book; in copious footnotes for almost every line. When puzzled I don't have to go rooting around for other sources. I have several excellent editions and translations of the Bible and many reference works, but for sheer convenience and comprehension that bulky Jerusalem Bible can't be topped.

Meanwhile, too, it seems that the more destructive critics hammer away at the Bible, the more scientific evidence emerges to authenticate its accuracy (far more than even most churches realize). Archaeologists keep discovering evidence that much of the Bible, too easily dismissed as myth or allegory, is literally true.

For instance:

. . . Nimrud, the biblical city of Calah, was found. . . . So was Nineveh, complete with the library and palace of King Ashurbanipal. And in the library ruins were clay tables which gave an eyewitness, supposedly Babylonian version of a vast flood too closely resembling the account in Genesis to be accidental.

Thirty years later Ur, the birthplace of Abraham, was brought forth in all its splendor by the British archaeologist Leonard Woolley. Six years of digging took him deeper and deeper until he came across layers of clean clay that could only have been deposited by water, and beneath that remains of a thriving civilization suddenly destroyed, cut off and sealed away by the layers of clay. He had found the flood! (From G. S. Wegener's *6,000 Years of the Bible*.)

. . . Many discerning people believe the Ark has been discovered. Or a craft remarkably similar in every detail to that described in the Bible. A six-hundred-foot, three-story boat buried intact in a glacier on Turkey's Mount Ararat, where Genesis said it would be: "And the ark rested in the seventh month . . . upon the mountains of Ararat." First sighted by two Russian aviators in 1916, just before the Revolution, sighted repeatedly by other pilots since. Actually visited by several expeditions that got close enough to take pictures. The French explorer Fernand Navarra and his son even drilled through the ice to pitch-saturated beams, bringing back pieces of hand-hewn wood that carbon-dated as being at least five thousand years old.

William Willoughby, religion editor of the Washington *Star-News*, says: "There is no evidence of any of them coming away less than fairly well convinced that the Ark is there, awaiting scientific confirmation."

. . . Scientists tell us it was possible for the whale to swallow Jonah, and for him to survive three days in its belly. Uncomfortable and certainly extraordinary, but possible.

. . . The discovery of the Dead Sea Scrolls in 1947 provided almost shocking evidence of the literal endurance of the Scriptures. The caves around Qumran, in the Judean wilderness, yielded more than four hundred manuscripts—ninety from one cave alone—representing every book of the Old Testament except Esther. Scholars poring over them have been able to settle many disputes and clarify doubts and questions.

. . . Prophecies, too many to list, are coming true every day. (Read Hal Lindsey's *The Late Great Planet Earth*.)

. . . The Mark of the Beast may soon become reality: "And he causeth all, both small and great, rich and poor, free and bond, to receive a mark in their right hand, or in their foreheads: And that no man might buy or sell, save he that had the mark, or the name of the beast, or the number of his name" (Rev. 13:16–17). Banks, complaining of too much paper work, have already devised and are in some places using a moneyless system whereby computers add to or subtract from bank accounts by numbers. Our government, together with the world bank, is trying to devise a plan to do away with currency altogether. To achieve it, each individual's identification number would have to be tattooed on hand and forehead.

. . . All this, and more. So much more.

So who is any one of us to challenge the Bible? I can only honestly admit I still don't understand a lot of it, how it happened or why it happened, but with God's help I'm making progress. And just because I don't yet understand does not mean it didn't happen, and that there weren't reasons beyond my poor human comprehension. After all, as G. S. Wegener says, "Essentially the Bible is . . . an account of God's dealing with man, and in the final analysis its truths spring from faith."

Faith. Such a little word to encompass so much. Does faith mean a blind and dogmatic rejection of reason? Does faith mean a kind of stupid submission to the dictates of anyone who claims to have a corner on all the truths in the Bible and I'd better believe his way? No, let's say that faith, for me at least, is a state wherein I stop quarreling with the Bible and start letting it speak to me on its own terms.

If I am seeking for flaws and inconsistencies, I can find them. But if I am seeking for truths and love and guidance, I can find those even more. I can find people of tremendous courage and dedication to their God, no matter where he led them or what dreadful things happened. I can find songs of praise and joy and wonder, and the outcries of tormented spirits asking the same questions we all ask: Why? *Why?*

I can find answers in the Bible. Every single life situation has its counterpart there, and the words for resolving its complexities. . . . I love the New Testament, which gives us Jesus, the total answer. I especially love the Gospel according to John wherein Jesus repeatedly asserts that he is the Messiah, the only begotten son of God. (I once tried to count the times but gave up, there were simply too many.) Not merely a prophet or a very good man, as many so-called intellectuals condescend (if such had been the case better to dismiss him as a charlatan or crazy!).

No, John was repeating these statements not as hearsay or speculation but because he personally heard them! He was the beloved apostle, Jesus' best friend. He was *there*. And so was Matthew, one of the original twelve. While Mark was a disciple (follower) who assisted Paul and Peter. And Luke a slightly later disciple who accompanied Paul on his journeys. So we have the four Gospels and the Acts and letters written by people who actually saw and knew Jesus, or were closely associated with those who did. And it seems to me the height of audacity—yes, gall—for other people centuries later to presume to discredit these eyewitness accounts. Radical skeptics frequently rationalize their arguments by assuming the New Testament wasn't written until many years after the events. Well, the letters were certainly current; the disciples couldn't have lived *too* many years after the Resurrection; and memories are long; and Jesus would have been a man hard to forget!

I love the Acts of the Apostles. I hadn't read beyond Acts for years and I had gotten the impression—how? where? from critics, liberal ministers—that Paul was an old curmudgeon who hated women, despised sex, and was something of a tyrant. But when I finally and somewhat dutifully read his letters, I found them enthralling. Such wonder at his courage, such affection welled up in me I could hardly contain it. What a man, what a writer! His concept of love:

> Though I speak with the tongues of men and of
> angels, and have not love, I am become as sounding
> brass, or a tinkling cymbal. . . . Love suffereth
> long, and is kind; love envieth not; love vaunteth
> not itself, is not puffed up. . . . (I Cor. 13:1, 4)

That entire thirteenth chapter of First Corinthians, surely one of the most masterful essays ever written on love.

And when he was under attack by his own, when he had already endured so much and could not take much more, he sat down to plead:

> Would to God ye could bear with me a little in
> my folly. . . . Thrice was I beaten with rods, once
> was I stoned, thrice I suffered shipwreck, a
> night and a day I have been in the deep;
> In journeyings often, in perils of waters, in
> perils of robbers, in perils by mine own countrymen,
> in perils by the heathen, in perils in the city,
> in perils in the wilderness, in perils in the sea . . .
> (II Cor. 11:1, 25–26)

My heart broke for him—this so very human saint.

Yes, if I am truly to find God and put my spirit at rest, I must seek him in that first and final word, the Bible. As I read somewhere, "When I'm thirsty, I don't want a formula, I don't want H_2O, I want water. So in my life I don't want just a book about Jesus, I want Jesus." If I am patient and open and uncritical, I will find him in God's own living account.

Work

And let the beauty of the Lord our God be upon us: and establish thou the work of our hands upon us; yea, the work of our hands establish thou it.

Psalm 90:17

To Love, to Labor

I am trying to find God.

Secretly, desperately, so many busy people are trying to find God. But we can't, we think we can't because we *are* so busy. Going to church to worship God takes time (precious time when we need to rest from all our busyness); meetings to talk about God take time. Prayers and meditation take time. . . . Peace, leisure, quiet . . . let me alone, give me a vacation away from my job and the family, let me walk along the seashore, climb a mountain, camp in the solitude of a forest. There I'll find God waiting and I can relax and say, "At last. I've been dying to meet you, have you over, come in!"

But the people of life keep clambering all over us, the business of life won't let us escape. Or if solitude, long postponed, is somehow achieved, are we comfortable with this stranger, God, are we sure he's even there?

No, no, if I am to know him, truly know him, neither of us can wait. What then? Take God along to work? *That* rat race? Absurd. Work is the result of God's enemy. Weren't Adam and Eve happy playing in the Garden (and walking and talking with God) until Satan ruined everything? They were driven out for their folly, and their punishment was to labor: "In the sweat of thy face shalt thou eat bread, till thou return unto the ground . . ." (Gen. 3:19).

So labor became a fact of life. The most important fact, actually, for most of us must work to survive. And work can indeed be punishment: work you detest, work that seems to be leading nowhere. But punishment is generally meant not to damage but to strengthen us. And that long-ago Lord of our beginnings knew it: No more handouts, no more childlike idling. . . . Toil, sweat, achieve, *grow*. . . . I made you, now make something of yourselves.

Back of that eviction curse lurked a blessing. The Creator was doing us all a favor, he was enriching the whole human race.

How glorious that you drove man from the Garden, God. How wise of you, how glorious! You saw that they would not have been complete in the Garden, undeveloped as children, playing children's games. You foresaw that they wouldn't have been happy, for there is no real joy in idleness, no challenge, no satisfaction.

Until they were forced to labor, procreate and labor, they could never become true people. Living, breathing, striving people, able to taste fruits far more sweet than that first forbidden apple: the fruits of their labor.

You gave them—and us—the gift of sweat, the salty baptism of our own toil. You gave us the sweetness of rest after a hard day's work. You gave us the satisfaction of accomplishment, the joy of a job well done. And you gave us goals, the dream of greater achievements to come.

And you foresaw that only in labor can there be love, true love. Man for woman, woman for man, and both of them for their children.

For we labor for those we love. And love sweetens that labor and the labor cements that love.

I can't imagine a world without work. Surely it would be an empty, meaningless world. A world without God in it.

To do the work you love, that is the main thing. To do work you realize you were born to do. Nothing can surpass that challenge, and if you succeed in it, ultimately reach your own soul's goals, then nothing can surpass that joy. When that time comes how easy to say, "God is with me, I have found God!"

But what of the people who have no burning conviction of their own life's purpose? What if I have no special talents, at least that I can see? Or what if, having them, even so I become trapped in some meaningless job? And what of the hated, uncongenial jobs along the way?

Much of what we do in life is less by choice than seemingly sheer blind chance. We need a job, we find one, we take it. By the time we begin to rebel—if we ever do—we are so often shackled by its security; there are mouths to feed. So life grinds on, grinding us back into the dust with it.

Is this God's will for us? Are we to submit, or struggle to escape? And what shall be the form of our escape?

Every day people go to work, herds and droves of people, often to dreary places to perform tasks they despise, or merely tolerate.

Every day throughout the world men, women—yes, and children—perform sheer brute labor. Where is the joy in this, where the blessing? Is the hand of God back of it all, guiding, sustaining, supporting, always holding open the door of our escape? Does God sink into the black guts of the earth with the miner and help hack the coal? Can he cool the fires of the blast furnace that roasts the steel worker, or help lift the waitress' heavy tray? What about the migrant worker and his family?

I don't know about the children; O dear God, I don't know about the children, except that the will in some of them is so strong they do eventually escape. . . . But this much I know: God is implicit in all that we do; God is there, awaiting our awareness. And by finding him, acknowledging his power to help us, we can escape—literally, physically, this place, this job, if that is truly best for us. Or escape simply the misery we endure because of it, misery that is often of our own creating.

For another of the mixed blessings involved in eviction from the Garden was free will. The soul is independent, it makes its own choices.

The Woman from the Mountains

There was this woman from the mountains.

We began to correspond when we were both young struggling writers. Her letters were novelette-length, hilarious and heartbreaking, about her life in a little Ozark town. She did all the cooking for her husband's truck-stop restaurant, baked hundreds of pies, cleaned and fried the chickens, gardened, canned, waited tables. She also ran the post office and sometimes delivered packages or important letters to remote cabins, precarious places which meant merry if painful misadventures and personal sacrifice. She was counselor and mother confessor to the truckers and most of the county.

She had one child, a little boy. Her husband was cold, often cruel, he failed to appreciate her. The townspeople took everything, gave back nothing—except gossip, pettiness, and scandal. Nobody read or listened to concerts, even on the radio. She was starved for love, art, intellectual companionship, the freedom really to write. . . . Thus she laughed and cried and raged within her prison.

After a series of these remarkably interesting letters, I suggested that since she hated the place, the work, and almost every person associated with it, she do as Betty MacDonald had done—take her child and go somewhere else, to write a kind of *The Egg and I* about her trials.

Her response? A sizzling twelve-page defense of all she had deplored!

Who did I think I was to propose abandoning a good man (despite his faults) and her obligations to all these decent if narrowminded people? There was absolutely no remedy for her problem, anyone could see that. Later maybe, when her child was grown, her husband less afflicted body and soul, the townspeople less dependent on her . . . Meanwhile, she was doomed to waste her gifts over a cookstove and counter. . . . But if this was God's will for her, by golly she would submit.

Duty. Honor. Loyalty. Obligation. Heaven knows we need those values, today more than ever. But it is now many years later. The son went off to college and married. The husband died some time ago. A superhighway put the restaurant out of business; the truckers go elsewhere. Yet, ignoring the door that has stood open so long it's banging on its hinges, my friend still stubbornly clings to the bars of her chosen cage.

God's will. Or our will? Who knows? For the soul is on its own secret journey, and there are lessons to be learned in every undertaking en route, however we resist. But surely if *our* will (for ourselves) is also God's will (for us), we can become truly reconciled. We will find something of sweetness and solace in the cup once thought to be so bitter. For God will be in it. A sense of his tremendous love and reassurance will be in it. We will find God closer than ever before.

Jobs I've Had and Hated

Nothing is ever unrelated in the marvelous life scheme. Everything has its purpose. I can look back now on some of the jobs I've had and hated (or thought I hated) and see their value and purpose. In retrospect there was no real suffering in them. I realize how trivial they seem compared to the conditions under which many people must work just to survive. But for me, for that time of my life, they were often grim and joyless.

The first one: clerking in the variety store of our little town . . .

Dread dogged every footstep toward that special prison of my Saturdays and holidays. Even now I seldom enter a dime store and breathe that special aroma—of gum and cosmetics and candy bars, of tennis shoes and cheap house dresses and school supplies—without feeling a half-tender shudder. . . . I hear again the screen door that squalled like a cat when opened, then snapped on people coming in and out. . . . Other kids buzzing about their dates and fights and who'd just been seen going into the movies with whom . . . Beyond, the sound of the Saturday night band concert thumping . . . the smell of popcorn and the lilac cologne of young farmers fresh from the barbershop . . . romantic excitement hovering, imploring, "Come out, come out!"

The sheer drudgery, the sore feet. My clumsiness in wrapping packages, my awful inability to find things. Mr. and Mrs. Strickler, who hired me, were very patient, very kind, but I groveled at my own ineptness, I walked in shame.

I learned other things, though. Lessons in kindness and patience of my own when it came to little old ladies intent on matching crochet thread, or children wanting to buy a surprise for their mother with only a few pennies to spend. I learned in new ways the lessons of scrupulous honesty taught at home.

The candy counter was a continual temptation. All those fragrant chocolates to be scooped up and weighed into the striped sacks. My mouth watered, but I knew that to yield even once would be disaster. I was a little puritan, I never took so much as a jelly bean.

One night I gave a woman too much change. For a ten instead of a five. Terrified, I dashed after her to the door, but she had vanished in the crowd. I turned back, heartsick, wondering how to tell the Stricklers (these were enormous sums then). I counted up how many Saturdays I'd have to work to repay those five dollars. . . . Then, just before closing, she returned, this gaunt little country woman, tagged by her barefoot children. Calling me aside so nobody would hear, she opened her shabby purse and counted out the ones.

She had to bite her lips, but her head was high. "We don't keep no money that don't belong to us," she said.

It was easier to pass the candy counter after that.

Other jobs . . . a series of small-town law offices as I worked my way through college (changing colleges halfway). Odd secretarial jobs for professors and registrars and deans.

Each prison has its special smell. . . .

The musty, closed-up smell of a small-town law office when you unlock . . . a dispiriting assault of varnish, leather, tobacco, and legal papers. Such a dry, dreary, *worry* smell, somehow . . . The odor of a college office is lighter, mellow yet crisp. The inky books and paper smell is sweet with age, lively with promise. As if you catch a whiff of some brisk if ancient brew forever in preparation for those who will partake . . . No, I never felt the same blunt despair unhooding a typewriter there. Yet it was imprisonment, nonetheless.

These vital jobs for which I was so grateful . . . the love-hate relationship I felt. Nobody ever treated me badly; it was just that I felt servile, a lesser thing, a tool to be used. . . . A paradoxical pride in work, though—the quick scamper of shorthand notes along the page, neatly typed letters and discourses and briefs . . . If you've got to do this, do it right. Slave, smile, endure (maybe he'll let me off early, please Lord don't let him keep me late). Serve your sentence until that blessed day when the books and desk and papers will be your own.

Were you there, God, all the time, though I couldn't see it? Was it your hand that pressed the buzzer, teaching me submission, yet rousing me to release? Was it your voice behind the droning, often maddening dictation? ("Patience. Serve this man with respect and care and patience; meanwhile, listen and learn.")

I was too young and untried, too new to myself and sketchily acquainted with God to realize he was there. Only now, looking back, I am astonished to discover the pattern of his guidance. Only now, mature, life-tempered, can I articulate some of the questions my own young heart was asking and that I have heard my children and others ask. Only now can I realize some of the reasons and understand some of the answers that God gives us when we cry out to him, assert our trust in him.

Why Am I Working Here?

This work you have given me, God. This job I seem doomed, at least right now, to do.

Why do I hate it sometimes, struggle so against its demands? Why do I so often drag myself to the appointed place and anticipate the day I must spend there as a form of penalty?

Why does it sometimes seem unworthy of me and the abilities you have given me? . . . Is this true, Lord? Is it unworthy, or am I unworthy of it?

Help me to sort out these confusions, God. To recognize, in a very practical, earthy sense, why I am performing this particular service during this particular time of my life upon the earth, and if it is really what you want me to do.

For I must find you in my work. Work is a part of life. You are a part of life—the very source of these hands, these feet, this brain.

Whether I am scrubbing a floor, pounding a typewriter, fixing a car, digging a mine, operating a machine . . . whether I am coping with personnel problems or an unruly classroom . . . I am earning my keep upon this planet, I am paying my way in human coin. And quietly, inflexibly back of the whole design, you are.

Is this seemingly empty, disagreeable labor a time of humbling? To show me I am of the selfsame stuff as my brothers and sisters— no worse, no better?

I, too, can lift and carry, argue, cope, hurt, get dirty, do things I dislike or things I consider beneath my so-called dignity.

Am I being tried for self-denial? Self-control? Am I being tested for appreciation? To be thankful that I have the means to earn my daily bread, and the ability to see its small but sure rewards (the shining floor . . . the ledgers that balance . . . the children progressing . . . the nuggets of coal).

Or is this a time of training, Lord? Of preparation for more vital challenges ahead? Of learning—every day, hour by hour, even though I can't see it—the skills and qualities I'm going to need?

This I know, Lord. This much I know and must remember: Nothing is wasted. Nothing is fruitless—no work that you give us to do. If it is of you—decent work, honorable work, work that helps mankind in any way instead of harming it—then that work is effective.

It affects my life's development, body and soul. And it affects everyone around me. My family; the people who work beside me.

And all the younger lives it touches, they are marked by my work, too.

Help me to realize this fact, to accept it and even glory in it. For now, for now, for as long as you really want to use me in this manner . . . But let me always be open to change. Alert for the voice that calls, "Come! You're ready for something else." Hopefully, something better. But at least the next step on the ladder of my life.

Until that time comes, I am resolved to return to my job rejoicing.

Giving more to it.

Getting more out of it.

Learning more from it.

And thanking you.

Which Boss Am I Working For?

No, God would not willingly lash me to a life of torment. He loves me too much; he has better use for me.

But how do I know? What are the signals?

This dread. This sense of futility . . . This waking in the night to accusing voices, reminding me of what I might have been . . . All my tactics of self-defense and compensation—the boasting, the pretending, the blaming of fate on others. I recognize them for what they are—an attempt to hide from my own failure. My secret shame.

When this becomes my lot, the message is clear, burningly clear: What I am doing is not right for me. Maybe once it was right, but no more. And if I am doing work that is truly wrong for me, then it is wrong for the world.

How can I illustrate? . . . Early in my career I wrote confession stories. We needed the money and they paid well. There was nothing actually evil or corrupting about them (compared to what's being published now they were Sunday school stories!). Yet after a while my spirit rebelled. I got tired of all that sinning, suffering, and repenting. And they were anonymous. One day a phrase from Dorothea Brande's book *Wake Up and Live* brought it all into focus. "Are you working at failure?" she asked. The answer was obvious. I was working for the wrong boss on a dead-end street. I withdrew from an assignment that would have meant a lot of money then, and slept well for the first time in weeks.

This is to cast no aspersions. Such stories are often beautifully written (I labored over mine as if I were trying to win a Pulitzer Prize). They may not be wrong for some writers, but they became wrong for me. I knew that I could and must reach a different, wider audience and for a different purpose.

If God is not in the work that I am doing, then I can't possibly find God while I am doing it. . . . Does that make sense?

The lady bartender who wrote to me . . . She had been encouraged and comforted by something I'd written. She gave a street address but didn't sign her name. I sent a reply, hopefully, just to the address, and received in return a long, heart-wrenching letter.

She was doing this to support her children. Tips made the pay excellent, but she worked in agony of soul. . . . The drunks, the unfaithfulness, the pickups, the language. Her own life was above reproach but she felt soiled, embarrassed for her children. It had never occurred to her to pray about the situation. But she began. En route to that bar she prayed, and she even prayed while there:

Lord, if you want me to keep on doing this, let me be a decent example to everyone while here; let me be cheerful, kind, sympathetic, understanding, especially to the lonely. . . . You yourself ate and drank with sinners. Who do I think I am all of a sudden?

Thus she reasoned and prayed and worked even harder at her job. And this sense of doing what she had to do *better* assuaged the anguish for a while. . . . Yet the torment returned, giving her no peace. She knew, at last, she had to get out.

She prayed for direction, then quit cold.

It was tough sledding for a while. Stopgap jobs—as a short-order cook, a salesgirl, a waitress in a diner . . . "But I felt free! I wanted to dance, hug my children, sing. And I could see the *sun*. I'd worked at night so long, slept so much by day, but now I was awake with the rest of the world, I could see the *sun!*"

And the family didn't suffer. The family itself was newly freed. Jobs and scholarships began to open up to them (was her own obvious release reflecting itself in the lives around her?) while she, the mother, took a course in hotel housekeeping and landed a place with a fine chain. . . .

Another case: the nurse who helped an abortionist. Those tiny bodies who had to be disposed of, some of them actually whimpering . . . those complete little beings whose lives had been stopped before they had a chance to live.

She hadn't thought she objected to abortion. She felt sympathy for women who conceived without meaning to and who didn't feel they could cope with the child. She felt she was co-operating in a service much needed. Yet face to face with the reality, she broke: "I can't do it, I can't. It's not right for me. God didn't give me the training, the gifts of help and healing for this!"

These voices of discontent and frustration—they are surely the voices of our own soul, God, searching for you, crying out for you, the God we have somehow lost in the business of making a living.

When this happens, surely the answer is clear: The work we are doing is not making a living but making a death!

"Is not the life more than meat?" you asked. "And the body more than raiment?" We dare not starve our souls for the sake of our bodies. We must eat, earthly food we must have. But that earthly food is not worth having if it poisons our souls.

Jesus also said, "No man can serve two masters."

How can we possibly fill the heart's deep hunger for God if we are actively engaged in the work of his enemy?

I realize that people who lock God out of their working lives aren't usually seeking him elsewhere. People who rob banks (or their customers or their neighbors), who push drugs (or a phony cure or worthless real estate), who sell their bodies in a brothel or their own children and mine to profit from pornography, who employ their health, energies, and talents in the thousands of ways available, often relish their occupations and couldn't care less about making contact with their Creator. (Sometimes they even fear and dread it, which is better than indifference.)

But there are also many people who try to compromise. Keep God in his proper Sunday morning compartment, safely away from things of which he would disapprove. Confess and be forgiven on Saturday, give generously on Sunday, and Monday back to business. . . . Are such people seeking to hang on to God through this arrangement, or only seeking appeasement? How do we know? Only God can judge. Whatever the motives, there is something childlike, frantic, and very sad about it.

Saddest of all are the people who recognize that their work is not only valueless but in many cases destructive, yet who feel trapped in it. God-haunted, despairing, they trudge day after day to the pointless and often evil waste of their precious waking hours. Too confused to pray, too honest to go to church, too insecure to change, they suffer.

Hear what their hearts are saying. Speak to them, rescue them, God.

Actually, doesn't it all add up to this? Each of us must ask himself: Which boss am I working for? Good or bad? God or the devil? God, the author and giver of life? Or life's defiler and despoiler?

And how can I tell? How do I know?

Surely I am working for God if my work is useful to other people. If it fulfills their rightful needs. If it helps rather than hurts. If it encourages, comforts, eases pain. If it makes their own work easier, brightens lives with laughter, teaches, guides, inspires . . . And my responsibility is greater if I have been given special talents.

I am not working for God if through my work, however "legal," I cheat my brothers and sisters, or damage them in body, mind, or their immortal souls. (And here, too, the responsibility is greater, my sin the graver if I have been given special talents.) God cannot go with me, be with me during such activities, so I am canceling God out of one-half my waking hours.

How then can I turn to God and reclaim him once I have washed my hands? I can't, not unless I grasp his own hand firmly and let him lead me to something else. Other work, a place and a way of life where I would not be ashamed to take him.

The Dirty Job

If the job is decent and useful, there really is no dirty job.

I can scrub floors, in my home or at an office; I can cope with garbage—at my sink or on a truck. I may not *like* to do it, but I will thank God I have the strength to do it. I will not consider myself too good to do it. I will not ask anyone else to do something I wouldn't do myself.

And I will discover rewards I might otherwise have missed.

Our son, the night when after much nagging he'd carried out the trash. (I'd done it all week.) "Mom, go look at the sky, it's unbelievable!" he exclaimed. Then, grinning, "Just think—I wouldn't have seen the sunset if I hadn't carried out the trash!"

Al Matthews, our rector—the day I surprised him in shirt sleeves at the church, a large can of refuse on his shoulder. His unassuming comment: "Oh, I always do this, I like to, it's one way of giving me humility; it reminds me I'm no better than anybody else."

And the inevitable comparison came: the night of the Last Supper. Jesus kneeling to wash his disciples' dirty feet. And how Peter protested, "Don't do that, Lord—oh, no, not you!" And Jesus' reply that we all must be equal, there is no high nor low in the Kingdom of God.

Remembering that, I can find God in the lowliest job I must do. I can wash a baby's diapers, empty a bedpan, cleanse a festering sore. I can gladly soil my hands and bow my back because God is in my heart, reminding me of the marvel of life in all its aspects, and the miracle of my own humanity.

Let No Job Be Beneath Me

Thank you, God, for the wonderful gift of work. Humble work. Hard work. Brain work or back work or hand work.

I don't care much for lily-white brains and lily-white hands. I like brains that have been toughened and tried. I like backs that have been strengthened and even bent by their burdens.

I like hands that are tough, too—wrinkled from water, calloused and bruised from rocks and shovels and hammer and nails. I like hands and backs and brains that have wrestled with things, lifted and carried.

Thank you that my parents worked hard and taught their children to work hard.

Help me to remember that no job is beneath me, and with your help no job will be beyond me.

Do We Work to Live, or Live to Work?

We must find God. We are groping for God so that our life will have some purpose. It is vital to feel that we were born for some purpose. And without God there can be no answer to the questions Why am I here? What am I *for?*

The answer has to lie largely in what we do with our lives.

Do. The very word connotes work. "What does he do?" means "for a living." And in a broader, deeper sense it is work that *keeps* us alive. When we no longer feel useful, productive, we die.

The beloved editor of my home-town newspapers . . . Still at it at ninety, wearing the same old green eyeshade. Years younger in body and spirit than retirees of seventy trying to fill their "golden years" with shuffleboard and checkers on the Courthouse Square . . . Then he sold out. I visited him six months later in the rest home, where it was as if a witch had been waiting to transform him into an aged stranger. He had shrunk. He trembled. In a few more months he was gone.

Bill Jarnagin with his newspapers . . . Pablo Casals with his cello. Picasso with his painting. And Maugham and Einstein and Shaw . . . And the peasants of the Russian republic Georgia, vigorously carrying their weight well past 100 (as old as 130 some of them claim), happy, venerated, *alive.*

Are idle people ever truly happy people? . . . Well, maybe mystics who withdraw from the struggle and spend their time in contemplation; maybe a few recluses and wanderers. But most of us need to be busy, whether at work we love or work we are forced to do.

True, we also need to rest. As a friend wrote when I had been going too hard: "Even the Lord rested on the seventh day, don't try to outdo him." We need times of letting go, relaxing, times of peace and meditation. But prolonged idleness leads not to rest but restlessness.

So I am grateful that I must work. It gives life meaning.

But now I must ask myself—do I work to live or live to work? . . . *Please, Lord, guard me against either.*

For if I work only to exist, then the work itself has no music, no meaning. And if I live only to work, then life itself has no significance, no savor.

To be truly happy and in accord with God's purpose, the work that gives me bread should also give me joy. Yet not so much satisfaction that it claims me totally, robs me of time for friends and family, the other delights of life. Then my work becomes my god. It is my work that I worship.

We all know people, generally men, who are always first at the office and last to leave, who are seldom home even weekends. "I'm doing this for *you*," the family is told. "So you can have more." (Less of me, but more material things.) The type is so common a name has been coined for them: "workaholics." Such absorption leaves little time for seeking God; rather, it is fleeing God. For God is love; and to flee one's loved ones, for whatever reason, is to deny them—and to deny the Creator of us all.

Often such men make a lot of money and achieve a lot of success. But the price is high. Often they lose their wives and families in the process; and all too often they are struck down at the very pinnacle of their success. Then work, instead of giving life, destroys life.

Goodness, how grim this all sounds! Because, when kept in balance, there is no greater blessing than to do the work you are suited for, and do it well. God has heightened it with so many rewards, hidden within it so many compensations.

And one of them is its power to release you from your troubles.

The Marvel

This is the marvel of work: that in the face of troubles you can do it.

The man is driven to distraction by events at home. Almost beside himself he leaves for his office. Yet there his responsibilities engulf him; he is caught up in that other world of his work which he must do. And, perhaps protesting somewhere inside himself, vaguely surprised—yet he can do it.

And the woman carries on with her work, as well. Particularly if she, too, works outside the home or is deeply involved in her profession. Yet even if she stays home, despite grief, conflict, worry, she washes the dishes and tidies the house and rises to the demands of

her children. Since these things don't take over the mind so completely, the woman often carries her wretchedness with her as she
goes about them; she can't dismiss it like the man or woman who
is forced to. Yet she can and does accomplish her duties.

And the writer. How often he or she must creep to the desk
to turn out words that are the very antithesis of private agonies.
Yet, amazingly, it is possible. The creative force within stills for a
little while the sound of suffering. The writer moves into another
world apart from it; his work rescues him.

The trouble doesn't necessarily vanish. Usually it is there patiently
waiting for any and all of us when we lay down our tasks. Like
some dark persistent lover it has not given up. Yet, curiously, after
the day's demands and accomplishments are behind us, we are
more equal to it. We can cope; we are tireder, yet somehow stronger.
As if the brief respite has refreshed us, given us perspective.

*Thank you, Lord, that work is such a powerful anodyne to pain
and problems. That in work we can both lose ourselves and find
ourselves.*

The Work I Was Born to Do

Thank God I know—knew from a very early age—the work I
was born to do. For me writing is less a profession than a compulsion. A calling. "Calling"—what a lovely word, fraught with so
much meaning. For inner voices do call, sometimes faintly, sometimes
fiercely—"Come, come, follow me."

Of course a lot of little voices try to join the chorus. We get
diverted, race this direction, that. (I wanted to be an artist,
too, to paint, perform; also to swim the English Channel.) But
there is no denying the true voice; our very soul recognizes it, and
there will be no peace unless we heed.

Often the true voice doesn't speak, at least not clearly, until
we have followed others. One of my nephews graduated from agri-
cultural college and was a county agent before starting all over in
law. Another had an advanced degree in aeronautics before God
called him, literally, in the night, to go to seminary and then to
Africa as a missionary. We all know ministers who were successful

in other careers before "answering the call." And men who gave up the ministry because it was simply not for them.

And we are familiar with stories of people who didn't discover their talents, or become outstanding in them, until late in life. (The classic example, Grandma Moses.) We also know of geniuses like Albert Schweitzer, who had mastered half a dozen arts before becoming a medical doctor and taking his skills into the jungles.

We know, too, sadly, that "many are called, but few are chosen." It is all too possible to hear the voice of what seems your heart's desire calling and yet be unable to live up to its requirements. Every career is so complex, each demands so frightfully much in dedication, sacrifice, sheer hard labor, and the ability to take its blows. The road to success (at least as the world thinks of success) in any field is littered with the bodies of people who were not as well suited as they thought or who simply lacked the stamina to survive. . . .

Three friends, all longing to be writers. Each had talent, each tried. But wanting "to be a writer" is far different from the merciless compulsion that drives one to write at any cost. After a while each went on to other distinguished careers. One became a pediatrician, one a decorator, one a lawyer. Each as difficult and challenging, but for the woman involved, her true calling.

Finally, there are thousands of people who are not strongly impelled toward anything. That's why guidance counselors and career specialists are so valuable. They turn on lights in the darkness for those who are groping, they help people find their way.

"And let the beauty of the Lord our God be upon us; and establish thou the work of our hands upon us; yea, the work of our hands establish thou it," says Psalm 90. . . . Then indeed there is beauty in life—when the work of our hands is established. Then indeed we feel the beauty of the Lord. For he is in it. We have the marvelous assurance we are doing the work we were born to do.

It needn't be great work, this work of our hands. It needn't make us rich and famous. But if it is of God, we will do it well and there will be joy and fulfillment in it.

A friend—Toni, the one who became the decorator—expresses it like this: "Anybody who sews or paints or fixes things is adding something to this world. Anybody who writes or creates music is doing the same thing. But you don't have to be an artist to be creative. You can create with hammer and nails and a piece of string.

"The main thing is to be useful. To make something other people can use and enjoy as well as yourself. And if you can make something that lasts, how wonderful. A house—to build a house for people to live in. Or to build a bridge for them to cross. A bridge is strong and often long and lovely in design, and if it's a good bridge, it will last for generations.

"I feel the same way about antiques. I love anything that is old and good. Some craftsman many years ago created this beautiful table that many people used before me and that my children and maybe my grandchildren will use and enjoy. Yet that man has been dead a long time, I don't even know his name. I just know he must have been a happy man, doing the thing he was born to do."

Another example. A Washington cab driver. One of the richest men I know. Jesus rides that cab with him, arms outspread. Jesus speaks through him in a daily witness of kindness and happiness. "I tries to make everybody feel a little better that rides with me," he says. "I prays for each fare I let out and I prays that the next person I pick up will be somebody that needs me." In case that need should be material, he keeps a supply of needles and thread, buttons, pins, tape, postcards, stamps—and waves off pay. He listens to confidences, cheers, befriends. No child leaves without a stick of gum and no adult without a word of encouragement and a little card that reminds: "Be happy, God loves you."

That man doesn't wake in the night to voices of self-contempt and accusation. In a city where there is so much fear and crime, so much grave responsibility, he knows God meant him to drive that cab. He is proud of bringing love to that job, the job he was destined to do.

Love to the job. That's it, isn't it? For God is love. When we love our calling, or even just bring love to the work we must do along the way, then God is in it. For his love gave us life and the need to work. And when we work with love we can find him.

Dedication

There is something more, though, and I must speak of it. There is dedication. A sense of commitment to your work so great you will endure great sacrifices for it, give it your all and a little bit more. A phrase meaning "I have worked hard," in the Lord's own language, Aramaic, expresses it well: "I have eaten my body and drunk my blood."

If your work is truly vital to you, then you will pour yourself into it, body, soul, and blood. Not to compete with anybody, nor for the money, nor for acclaim. But out of a sense of fulfilling your personal mission. Your God-given purpose. And far from separating you from God it will be a form of worship. Of communion. Of knowing you are truly one with him and he is one with you.

Don't let me ever leave you out of my work, Lord, or get too busy for you. Let me always remember you are the source of my work, and every reward that it brings to me.

Be with me every working hour, making that work better. Making the world a better place because of it, and me a better person whose work brings me closer, ever closer to you.

Nature

The heavens declare the glory of God; and the firmament sheweth his handywork.

Psalm 19:1

The Earth's Heart Beating

How can I find you, God? How can I claim your strength?

I am tired, so tired . . . tense, so tense. And my nerves are screaming. Now, if ever, I need you. I need your reassurance and your peace.

Yet there is only this raw trembling vacancy inside me. This sense of emptiness and futility.

Come back to me, Lord. Calm me, quiet me, for I am indeed weary and heavy-laden and I need your promised rest.

"Stop going so hard, Mother," a daughter says. "Lie down a few minutes, relax."

I flop on the floor and she kneels beside me, long and lithe and fair, and deftly massages my neck and back. "Let yourself go. Be like the cat."

It dozes on the arm of a chair, eyes half closed. I stretch out . . . and out . . . trying to emulate its yawning movements. . . . How utterly cats yield every muscle and nerve, how sweetly they sleep. But how do they occupy themselves all day? I wonder. Nobody to play with, nobody to talk to, nothing to think about. Yet this cat of ours goes outside and vanishes for hours . . . must surely occupy itself with something for hours. Chases a bird or a rabbit, suns itself, prowls the woods . . . How stupendously boring—unless you are a cat.

I ponder some of this aloud, and my daughter, who has left my side, looks up from the jeans she is mending.

"She's in tune with the universe," she says. "God keeps her happy."

"Why? I wonder. Why a cat at all?"

"God put her here to be company to us, and perhaps to teach us that. That the way to be happy is just not to worry, to relax, to flow with the universe."

"But people can't do that. We have too many problems, things to worry about."

"Yes, but the animals have their problems, too," she says. "Most

of them. The mere problem of survival. And they're calm about
the whole thing, they trust nature—their own nature and the larger
nature all around them."

"People are different. We can't be like that."

"Yes, we can. Some people do. People who take up the religious
life and just meditate, or take vows of silence. It's the same thing,
just merging with the universe."

"That seems selfish. It's escaping responsibilities to other people."

"I think nature meant us to be more selfish than most people
are. What's really more important than the self, Mother? You
yourself? The problems go away, most of them, but you remain.
You stay *you*. You shouldn't let yourself get so damaged and
divided up by responsibilities and problems."

Thoughtfully she bites a thread. "I pray about things, so many
things, so many problems. I know I don't have half so many responsibilities as you—yet I think I have a lot, for my time of life I
do. And I pray about the people and the problems, and then I try to
meditate, but that takes mental effort. It's better when I just let go,
just relax and let myself flow into nature—the rain, for instance. The
rain speaks to me almost as if it's trying to tell me something. Last
night it was raining and I prayed and pretty soon it was the rain
praying with me, and almost the rain praying *for* me. I could just
lie there and listen.

"And there are times when I have just lain out in the sun and
on the grass and flowed into it, the universe—and I could hear the
earth's heart beating."

"The earth's heart?"

"Yes, don't you think God put some of his own heart into the
earth when he made it? And gave it a heart, too?"

(Out of the mouths of babes, I think . . . or a daughter twenty-
two . . . No, wisdom is not reserved solely for the old.)

The earth's heart beating . . . and my own. Yes.

For now as I lie here resting, yielded as the cat, it comes to me
through my own hand, that steady pulsing . . . and hers . . . and
that of the quiet cat.

For are we not all one? Linked to the same rhythms, we three
creatures within this room . . . and all those beyond. Seen and unseen, the blood flows, life-sustaining.

Within the very earth itself the currents flow. The vital life forces of all its inhabitants and the saps and juices of all its vegetation reaching down and up. And in and through and deeper, ever deeper, the ceaseless silent pounding of energies undreamed.

A sense of joyous discovery fills me.

For I realize now that to sense it and become one with its source I must stop struggling. To fight with life is to fight off God!

Now I feel his presence, his reality, his strength.

Now I hear the quiet rhythms and am cradled in those rhythms like a child being rocked to sleep. . . . Now I can truly rest.

A Potato

I am peeling a potato.

What a homely thing it is, this lumpy ellipse in my hand. Brown, earth-brown, with the dust of the earth clinging to it. Yet as my knife strips away its humble skin, how moistly pure and white it is inside. Solid yet succulent, rich with the nourishment drawn from the darkness in which it lay.

Contrasts—all these contrasts. The light and the dark, the buried and the risen. The continuing miracle ready to spring from the ordinary things of everyday . . . How amazing this is. What secret treasures the silent soil holds. And how little we have to know and be to tap them . . . A potato! This potato.

If I were to save even a chunk of it, a piece with an eye in it, and bury it, it would become another plant bursting forth with leaves and flowers to inform me when it was ready, that it had flung about it hidden nuggets to be dug. Offering me more potatoes than I would need for a week . . . Such abundance!

And such magic. That this mealy whiteness soon to feed my family emerged from the mute black stuff beneath my feet. Dirt, plain dirt. Dirt that we get on our shoes and are forever trying to drive out of our houses. Low, common, spurned, yet vital to the whole life plan, and during this existence, at least, never to be escaped. It upholds me every step I take. And though I may fly from it by plane and flee from it by boat, it is the substance to which I must always return. I am earth-bound. Chains of gravity hold me to the earth, and the even more powerful chain of life itself. Its grains and its grasses feed me, and so do its trees with their nuts and fruit. Except for fish, every creature that nourishes me likewise must draw its own nourishment from the earth. While deep in its body it carries fuels to warm me, minerals and elements to build and serve me in a thousand ways.

Scientists in their laboratories might be able to duplicate synthetically all its elements. They can and have made artificial substances in which things will grow. Yet what of the organisms that exist in that soil, the microbes, the bacteria, the bugs and worms? Even a teaspoon of soil. A thimbleful, a pinch. In *The Secret Life of Plants* the authors tell how the famous oceanographer William Beebe occupied himself during a long sea journey by analyzing a small bag of earth mold. "And found in it over five hundred separate specimens of life. He believed that more than twice that many remained to be identified."

Soil squirms and breathes and lives, it draws life into itself and gives life back.

And so—this potato . . . Brown with the same earth from which human beings came, and the earth to which we must return.

I think of Genesis. First two chapters. Turn the fire low and read them. . . . The simplicity. The absolute directness and purity of the story of creation. God so busy about his monumental task:

> And the earth was without form, and void; and
> darkness was upon the face of the deep.

Try to imagine. I can't. But God (or something) imposed order. Brought light, divided night from day and sea from land.

> And let the dry land appear: and it was so.

> And God called the dry land Earth; and the gathering
> together of the waters called he Seas: and God saw
> that it was good.

> And God said, Let the earth bring forth grass, the
> herb yielding seed, and the fruit tree yielding
> fruit after his kind, whose seed is in itself, upon
> the earth: and it was so.

And the earth brought forth grass, and herb yielding
seed after his kind, and the tree yielding fruit,
whose seed was in itself, after his kind: and God
saw that it was good.

There is something very tender and moving about that. Someone,
or something, wanted things to be so right for us. Everything in
readiness and plenty of it—so much, so much. And when every
last thing had been done, he took a bit of dust from the ground:

and breathed into his nostrils the breath of life;
and man became a living soul.

I once dismissed all this as a pretty myth. But only out of my
own ignorance and futility, my helplessness to understand. I tried
to replace it with formulas and theory (I didn't understand those
either, but I thought they sounded more intelligent). Now I see that
it is really more intelligent to acknowledge the marvel as simply
beyond understanding. But that someone or something indeed "saw
that it was good." Not chaos but order. Not poisonous but life-
sustaining. And the most remarkable creation of all emerged from
the mystery: man with his mind and his choices and his indestruct-
ible soul.

There is something tender and moving, too—and to me almost
funny—that this Creator chose the dirt for our source. Why not a
drop of water or the petal of a flower? Nothing so delicate or
aesthetic—no, a bit of the rich yet humble dust! . . . So I am akin
to this potato and everything that grows. For this dust, this very
dust that I am rinsing away right now, provides all the building stuff
of my body. And when that body is no more use, it will return to the
ground.

Strange.

Allegorical language has a way of distilling and preserving deep
instinctive truths. We speak of the good earth, Mother Earth. And
we call God our Father. The one who created this earth and richly
seeded her to produce this whole family I belong to—the family
of man. We are indeed children of the earth, as we are children of
our earthly parents. And all this makes us children of God.

The Trees

We seek you in people, God. We try to find you in churches; we hunt you diligently in books. And all the while your reality is everywhere around us, simply awaiting recognition. Your messages are written in the landscape if we'll only look.

Brother Lawrence, the seventeenth-century monk who left such a beautiful legacy in his *Practice of the Presence of God,* was converted by the mere sight on a midwinter day "of a dry and leafless tree standing gaunt against the snow; it stirred deep thoughts within him of the change the coming spring would bring. From that moment on he grew and waxed strong in the knowledge and love and favor of God."

Years ago in suburban Philadelphia . . . my tree. A great oak whose branches scraped the attic window where I had fixed up a cubby with books and papers. My cozy high retreat. There I could sometimes flee when the storms of life seemed almost too much to bear. . . . Lie across the couch "having a good bawl," as my mother used to say. Grappling with a woman's private agonies . . . Mine, rejection slips piled as high as the dishes in the sink . . . The daily tearing asunder as children, desperately loved, wove maddeningly in and out of my study with their tears and little treasures and demands . . . A husband I was lucky to see once or twice a week . . . And now this—after three years of editorial encouragement and personal sacrifice, the return of the novel that would (I thought) solve everything.

Rain pouring down to match my tears . . . The plaintive screech and scratch across the glass, then tap-tap-tap as if something was begging to come in . . . Go fling up the window, break off the offending branch. Yet there with the coldness on my face, something held me. Some majesty of motion—this greater thing than I swaying and keening and uttering its own cries into the wind. Its permanence spoke to me, its great age. It had lived long before me and would go on living, no doubt, long after I was gone. Blind, deaf, unfeeling, how could it know anything about me? And yet it spoke to me, comforted me in a way I could not articulate.

Later, when it was dark, I remember going down and putting on a son's old hooded mackinaw and creeping out in the rain to embrace that tree. Self-dramatics? Maybe. But I wanted to put my arms around its great girth, feel its bark against my cheeks. It had something to give me no human being could. Just what, I didn't know. Only that it stirred in me some deep sense of protection and faith. God, my long-neglected God, had created that tree.

If he could do that, he could do anything! He could look after me.

These moments of awareness, Lord. These powerful moments of conviction. Why can't we hang on to them? Why do we let them slip away?

Yet they are not in vain. Looking back, we remember them with a kind of puzzled wonder. Looking forward, even during the times when we feel hopelessly lost and groping, something tells us they will come again.

And if we will listen, truly look and listen, there is no stopping them. They will happen over and over.

They will happen now!

God has so much to say to us through the trees. Lie on your back and read his eloquent sermons in the trees. . . .

A chill but sun-gilded February day. I stretch out on a wooden bench in the yard and gaze up at the sky. And all about me rise the trees, naked, stripped, revealed. They are like nude dancers stretching . . . stretching . . . glorying in their lovely bones. How incredibly tall they are and how straight they grow. The trunks in almost every cluster soar unswerving toward the sky, as if intent upon their goal. Yet their branches reach out . . . out . . . a little uplifted as if in adoration or rejoicing. They are in an attitude of dancing or of prayer. And I see that they are open, so very open, as if to give and to receive.

What blessings pour down upon those grateful arms. Sun and wind and snow and rain and lighting wings. They are merry with squirrels; and at night they wear stars in their fingers.

They are open for giving as well. They are lively with birds, they hold their nests for safekeeping. Soon these outstretched arms will be bursting with buds and flowers and leaves. They will spread their fragrance and their shade. Nuts will rain down from these generous arms, fruit will clot their branches and be claimed by other arms, upreaching. Or the fruit will fall by its very abundance, too much for the boughs, so richly receiving and giving, to contain.

And it is all a matter of the sturdy central trunk, undiverted on its skyward journey, yet accompanied, always accompanied by these happy, open, spreading arms. . . .

The design—the perfect design for tree or man. To be strong in central purpose, heading toward the destination meant for us, but open, always open both to give and to receive.

Water

"And the Spirit of God moved upon the face of the waters."

And the waters have drawn us ever since.

Water . . . Our earliest, most primal memories are of water, in the mother's womb. Then we are bathed, given water to drink, and the lifelong thirst begins.

God leads me to the water. I feel the constant tug. . . . Water called out to me before I can remember, for I was born on the shores of a big Iowa lake. . . . That enchanting, heaving mystery below . . . struggling to touch it, taste it, possess it, but strong arms hold you safe . . . Smell of fish and bait, clank and creak of oars. The mesmeric bobbing of a tiny cork. "Now sit very still and watch it," Grandfather says, fitting your hands to a bamboo pole. . . .

Peeling off shoes and stockings to wade—chill softness around your ankles, sand between your toes . . . And the ultimate ecstasy, plunging in, merging, though it meant fire up your nose. Again strong arms hold you, sustain you as you struggle, then you are released . . . the miracle is happening, you are free, free, one with the water now—swimming!

We swam and dived like water rats all summer, survived the harsh winters, and haunted the banks in spring, as if the very urgency of our yearning could hasten the melting of the huge ice boulders. We were always first in, last out, and often our mother paced the floor. . . . Meanwhile, the pageantry of the sky, doubled by its reflections. Scarlet sunrises and golden sunsets. Northern lights, the Milky Way. And ladders of blazing stars that rivaled Jacob's (you had only to step out from the dock to climb them straight to heaven). Giant calendar-picture moon paths paved with crushed diamonds . . .

A lake intensifies, multiplies. Heady with youth and love, we wallowed in all this beauty, never questioning its source. The heavens *did* declare the glory of God, and the firmament around Storm Lake, at least, was evidence of his handiwork.

Then I went away to college. And got married.

Was it the moving that dimmed your reality, God? Was it that as much as the inevitable growing up? Was it the subtle but cruel separation from a source of self that had to do with water? . . . City streets and city buildings riddling the sky. City smoke and rush and grime and noise. City apartments with people quarreling on the floor below and music rattling the dishes in the cupboard. Even the cold fascinating face of city sophistication.

All this blotting out your face, blasting out of existence the sense of acceptance and communion. Did that have a lot to do with it, Lord?

I don't regret the going. Life can't remain a childhood pastorale forever. Not for most of us. Isn't the voice of your own destiny the voice of God calling, too? Go charging forth to follow, wherever it leads. And if your faith is strong enough, God's reality goes with you. Mind was simply too blithe and shallow. Foolish as it sounds, it had something to do with water. And I was cross and vain and lost and confused.

Psalm 42 could have been written for me:

> As the hart panteth after the water brooks, so
> panteth my soul after thee, O God.

> My soul thirsteth for God, for the living God:
> when shall I come and appear before God?

> My tears have been my meat day and night, while
> they continually say unto me, Where is thy God?

Repeated transfers. Moves about the country. For years I didn't mind, looked forward to changes, always liked the last place best. Yet beneath the superficial cheer lay this sense of being parched, body and soul; and always this desperate hope that next time there would be water. . . . Twice we settled on little streams, and my heart coasted down like a bird and was briefly at rest. Just to look out the window and see that shining ribbon—how cleansing, healing. It seemed to wash away deeply imbedded fears and concerns, the very sight was soothing. And to hear its lilting voice . . . mocking misery, laughing at crossness and complaints.

To wade with the children. To lie on a sunny bridge watching the waving fingers of mosses, and the silver minnows darting . . . stones glittering, sun-stars exploding . . . to listen to the busy thump and chirp of frogs and crickets and all the myriad life forms water draws . . . The presence of God comes back in a warm golden flooding. Questionings melt away. There is only this sense of harmony and oneness.

If only such hours could last. I think it very possible that getting back to water sooner would have hastened my total reunion with God.

Finally, after further wandering in the wilderness like the Jews, we were led to this Virginia lake. Lake Jackson. A small lake compared to the lake of my beginnings, yet a broad bright vista of water that winds through hills and lush green woods for twelve miles. Here we have had a summer home for years, and here I found God waiting.

You are there, Lord, when I wake up in the morning.

A little shout of recognition springs up in me, a cry of joy and wonder. Water has reclaimed me. You have reclaimed me!

Out of the dark sluggish nest of sleep I come, into the breaking light, reborn.

Grayness is melting to rose. Softly, softly the whole world is abloom in a soft pink glow as bare feet pick their way down cold rock steps for the day's first swim. The flowers and grasses are heavy with dew; birds are belling and chiming in the trees. A white smoke of mist is rising from the water . . . the dawn of creation. Plunge into it, fiery baptism, sense-assaulting. . . . Swim . . . swim! Motion makes your own blood warm you, like good wine.

The mists wreathe softly all about, blurring and powdering the dimly sensed shape of trees. It is like plowing through the landscape of a dream. . . . No, it is like flying. Sweep low, rise high, roll and coast and give yourself over to this liquid loveliness. (Do the birds feel thus, or the angels trying out their newfound wings?)

Tired, I tread water. The mists have lifted, my chin is level with a sparkling expanse. And I turn in a little circle of wonder, surrounded by broad glassy meadows ignored or undiscovered—they are mine, all mine, I can claim them for my own. . . . I lie on my back and claim the sky, too, so vast and entrancing in all its moods. One day cloud-strewn, another vivid linen-blue. And the water crisply mirrors every cloud and bird and the lovely leaning trees.

The lake seems as vast as the sky which embraces the universe. These two parallels, lake and sky, reach out to each other, merge. And I, in the middle, seem somehow a link, as if they are fused within my body, as if in the act of swimming and gazing up I am joining them in me. My own silent being. They are a part of me and I of them, and we are all one with God.

The water supports me. I think of the everlasting arms—especially when floating. For years, though I could swim and dive I couldn't float. The trick of relaxing and just trusting the water to hold me up escaped me. Like Peter who started to walk to Jesus, I was all right until I became afraid. Then panic and struggle and sinking. When I stopped fighting—just when I don't remember—and gave myself over to the strong liquid muscles beneath, it was simple.

Is joining God like that? Is coming to God like that?

Lord, you beckon and we start out so bravely . . . then we look about us and get scared. . . . The crazy world chopping and churning all about us . . . our own awful weaknesses and failures, our self-disdain, our doubts.

Only when we keep our eyes on you, reach out our hands to you in absolute trust, are we safe.

The Cows

I don't need to seek God in nature, for he is there. Every sunrise testifies to his presence, every rainfall, every flower. It is impossible to stand by the sea and watch the waves rolling in without being almost overcome by a sense of his wonder, or see the wind lashing the trees without feeling his power.

And in nature I have learned lessons about God's own nature. They are written in the landscape, they are hidden yet ready to be discovered in the flight of birds or the very stance of trees. And secrets have been unlocked for me simply by observing his creatures, some of the answers to the eternal riddles of existence have been revealed.

I began to understand free will (at last!) on a creek bank one day, watching the cows. Five or six stood cooling themselves in the water, jaws busy, eyes bland. What a fixed stare cattle have. A kind of blank brooding. Their tails kept flicking flies off their backs, their jaws never ceased their silent rhythms. As we first approached, a couple of them emitted blasts of sound that sent the children scurrying. (A cow's moo is not a gentle thing, and musical only in stories.) Now they simply stood regarding me where I had stretched out on an army blanket.

The children were off trying to catch crawdaddies in a can. I lay alone resting, reading, gazing into the sky or returning the empty stare of the cows. . . . Overhead, clouds coasted, a hawk wheeled, and to the west I could glimpse a V of geese and faintly hear their honking. . . . How free the geese, I thought, how earth-bound and fated the cows.

Other birds called from the trees. What were they saying? I wondered. And what message had there been in the bellow of the cows? . . . Poor cows, blatting their foolish protests, now resignedly silent. Cows to be milked morning and night, or herded onto trucks and hauled off for slaughter. How sad to be a cow. If I had to be another creature and could choose, I'd join the wild geese flying. How free, how free! . . . But wait, the geese aren't free either. They fly always in formation and to certain feeding grounds at certain seasons. And their entire vocabulary is limited to that honking I hear faintly, thrillingly now. How sad to be a goose, speech-deprived.

And it occurs to me that human beings are the only creatures equipped with words. Why? Why were all the marvels of language reserved for us alone?

These cows. These birds. Not only the geese but the bobolinks singing from the pasture grasses, the turtle doves mourning, the other little voices chipper or sleepy in the trees . . . They are telling each other something, no doubt, they are expressing something. For almost every creature, bird or beast, has a voice with which to court, proclaim hunger, anger, fear, pain, and joy. And so, in a small and limited way they can communicate with each other and with us.

Yet they have no vocabulary, there is no way with which they translate their thoughts, if thoughts they have. They can't read, they can't write. They miss the entire experience of books and poetry and plays. . . . These books I have brought with me, to read or not. A cow couldn't choose; a bird could only peer over my shoulder, a butterfly poise on the pages, not understanding. Why should they? They have no need for the secrets locked in those letters.

The alphabet. Such a tiny package, less than a handful of letters to reveal such vast treasures: Words! Millions of words, not only in my own language but in the languages of the world. All but a few use this same alphabet. This magical key which I, as a person, own as a birthright and can use to my heart's delight. For I have been given the mind to understand it; and I have the sole choice what I shall speak, what I shall read, what I shall learn.

I can turn my back on knowledge and move dumbly through life like a cow, or I can open books and become transported in time and space. I can learn anything I want to in the whole wide world.

So as I lie in the shade beside that stream contemplating our differences—the cows' and mine, the birds' and mine—it dawns on me that herein lies the answer to something that long has troubled me: free will. In creating us as independent beings and sending us into life equipped with one simple tool God indeed made us "only a little lower than the angels." With dominion over the animals—and over ourselves.

That's it. That's got to be it!

For the animals aren't free. "Free as the birds," we say. Yet these very geese, flying in formation, are driven toward their destination by forces beyond their control. The bright singers in the trees—all, all function not from choice but from instinct. Even animals still living in the wild have been programmed to their ways, they needn't choose. Creatures of every other kind are trapped, usually within a single environment, during their brief life-span. Even their journeys, if they make them, are performed by instinct rather than choice, or by the choice of man. Animals can have neither dreams nor aspirations. They can't decide to work or not, or choose between the jobs they have (not even beavers or bees or ants). They can't invent things to make life easier. They can't benefit themselves by education; if they are trained at all, it is by man, and for the use and pleasure of man.

By comparison, how free we are. Trapped between birth and death, yes, but able to make so many choices in between. To do with our lives what we will. Average people—in a free society where there are no human dictators to force us—we can work where we please at whatever we please, marry whom we please, travel wherever we want.

Laws impose a few limits on us, there are social limits of our own devising, and we consider ourselves limited sometimes by lack of money or by the environment that seems wrong for us. But there is no force in existence that keeps us from breaking those limits, even of law. Unlike the animal kingdom, our Creator gave us free will. We can be as good or as bad as we want. As wise or as ignorant. We are free to move about and try things, accepting, rejecting, shaping the pattern of our days.

And when we are tempted to ask why God doesn't step in and intervene to spare us wars and murders and rapes, all the misfortunes that befall us, we must not forget that such intervention would be bought at the cost of forgoing our greatest gift of all.

We would then become as the animals. Free and yet not free. Free from the bother of making choices, from the penalties involved when we err. But herded about like cattle, dumb and wordless about our fate. Isn't it better, surely, to write the story of our own lives in a language freely given us? Our follies, our mistakes, the countless times of anguish caused by our very choices—surely even these are better than to live the bland life of a beast.

And this, too, has drawn me even closer to a personal reasoning God. If I could conceive of a universe populated only by animals— yes, it might possibly be considered some kind of mysterious, still awesome accident. . . .

But the fact that we, too, are here, Lord, your people, thinking, speaking, laughing, choosing, falling, rising, loving—that can be no accident. Thank you for creating us in your image, and releasing us on this remarkable planet with complete freedom to live the lives you have given us.

The Church

For where two or three are gathered together in
my name, there am I in the midst of them.

Matthew 18:20

Upon This Rock

I must think about the church. I must ask myself, How much do we need the church? When it comes really to finding God, leading people back to God, how much does the church help? And *does* it always help?

I think some people run screaming from the thought of God because it seems to conjure up a sudden awful obligation to go to church. . . . No, no, I like things as they are—to sleep late Sunday mornings and drink coffee and read the New York *Times*. Or to get up early and play golf. Sunday's my day of rest and recreation; after slaving all week I just don't want to do anything I don't have to. It's my life, doggonit, so go away, miserable nagging voice of duty or conscience, stop bugging me!

If getting together with God means having to get up and dress up and march into a building with a lot of other people, forget it. It's too much like school, like parents ordering, "Do this, do that." And it brings back too many memories—dear memories, some of them— Mother playing the organ, Dad dozing in the back pew . . . but sad memories, too . . . funerals . . . the hymns, many of them so doleful. And the ministers often speak in phony tones; bright and normal when making announcements about choir practice and the bazaar, but going suddenly absolutely sepulchral when reading from the prayer book, sonorous in the sermons.

And all the activities, the vigorous time-consuming activities. I want God, I want God—not a rummage sale or a pancake supper or a card party or Bingo. Not even the "social involvement" of what to do about integration and women's rights and politics and war . . . All this confusion, this sheer human confusion, trapped within the framework of an institution called Church.

Does God demand all this of us if we are truly to know him? Is the framework absolutely necessary? . . . Let me think about this. I'm not sure—I wish I were. Let me think about Christ.

He did speak of his church. When Peter said, "Thou art the

Christ, the Son of the living God," Jesus responded, "Upon this rock I will build my church."

Church. What kind of church did he mean? There were synagogues in those days, and the Temple. He preached and taught in them, but most of his ministry was on hillsides and by the sea and on the streets. Multitudes followed him and listened enthralled. Fishermen put down their nets and listened. Serving men put down their trays. The sun beat down, the hot winds blew in their faces . . . the waves rolled in, overhead the stars sparkled.

These great gatherings of people drinking in his amazing words. Words of admonition, yes, but words of love, words of hope. Words that spoke profoundly and with tremendous authority of his own divinity and the precious individual value of each human soul. Words that told us exactly what we must do to be one with God.

And so the Lord was surrounded by all these people, his living "church." But there were times when he must escape. He had to replenish his own spirit. He could not continue healing and inspiring and leading without direct personal contact with God. Warning his disciples not to tell where he was going, he went off alone to pray. To a garden, a mountaintop, a body of water. Sometimes he prayed all night.

But in the end, when he hung on the cross, they stood by him. They kept the vigil, the faithful ones kept vigil. His "church." And I think now of the little band of the faithful who don't abandon you when you need them today. Let sickness come, let tragedy strike, let death invade the home and the church appears. No matter if you've been near their door in years, no matter if you even belong. The church says, "We're here, we'll help you."

My husband's first heart attack: We were new to the neighborhood, hadn't bothered yet to join a church. Yet a call was waiting when the ambulance reached the hospital. A Mr. Matthews? But I didn't know any Mr. Matthews. . . . He was the rector at St. John's, his wife told me when I picked up the phone. A parishioner had called him, he was already on his way.

Without some kind of organization how can such things be?

I think, too, of that first church struggling to survive, to find its own identity after its Christ had disappeared. The people had to gather someplace. How else could they discuss what he had taught them and try to figure out what to do next? There had to be meetings where they could share Paul's letters and read the Scriptures and pray and worship together. Sometimes they turned to each other for sheer protection in the face of persecution—whippings, torture, imprisonment, unspeakable deaths. Fear of a common disaster strengthens brotherhood; their very tribulations made them cling to each other with an intensity of love and faith, and out of these bonds they fashioned what they called their church.

But something happened to that first simple, impassioned faith. Between those humble, desperately dedicated beginnings and today— centuries of complex and preposterous happenings. Wars and crusades and inquisitions. Incredibly—in the name of the one who had said "Be merciful" and "Do not judge"—Christians doing the persecuting and torturing. Christians doing the killing! . . . And though the Lord had also said, "Blessed are the poor" and "Sell what thou hast and give to the poor" and "Feed my sheep"—splendid, richly appointed buildings rising, while people starved. And a hierarchy of men wielding authority and power, men in ornate trappings—though Christ had walked the dusty roads like a tramp, not knowing even where he might sleep. Though he commanded his twelve apostles as they set forth two by two: "Take nothing for the journey except a staff—no bread, no haversack, no coppers for their purses. They were to wear sandals but, he added, 'Do not take a spare tunic'" (Mark 6:8–10, Jerusalem Bible).

No, no, I must not dwell on these things. I must not hold the church accountable for all the sins of the past. If I am to come to know God, I must learn forgiveness. Forgiveness of others. Forgiveness of myself. *I must forgive the church!*

Yet these memories . . . aren't they perhaps part of a common guilt? A preternatural uneasiness that can't be easily eradicated. Because—for some of us at least—they get entangled with other depressing, disagreeable residue: Now get up, hurry up, come on, we can't be late . . . hell-fire, damnation, evangelists thundering doom . . . don't play cards, don't go to movies, especially on Sunday, and what if the Lord should come back and catch you at a dance?! . . . and bake sales and fund drives—you've got to give more, you've got to help. . . .

How can it *not* be this way? Poor confused people trying to hang on to God. Poor, hard-working, earnest people desperately trying to keep the organization functioning . . . Does the person seeking God want to get involved in what seems to him so much self-inflicted mutual misery?

Poor people. Poor *church*. Especially today as it struggles to find itself, going through rebirth pangs in some ways more tortuous than the throes of the early church. For its God was not dead—he was just being born, bloodily but triumphantly. They believed in him, rejoiced to die for him . . . they *believed*.

But now—now . . . this confusion, not only in the church but among many of its leaders. Who write articles for hedonistic magazines like *Playboy,* questioning the old moral values as irrelevant to our times no matter what the Bible states. (Maybe we need a new Bible?) Who lead riots and uprisings, who break into the offices of draft boards and chemical plants and destroy other people's property. Bishops and teachers in seminaries who don't believe in the basic precepts of their own church (the Virgin birth, the miracles, the resurrection). Well, I didn't either for a long time, but I do now, and if I'm going to identify with the Christian church, I don't want anybody mixing me up just because he's mixed up himself.

There is a terrible honesty, though, in the church's self-examination. Its self-flagellation for its failures, its noble and agonized search for justification. Its experimentation to find new forms of worship that will really speak to a tragically alienated generation. And to find some answers, not only some sane solution for racial conflicts and wars, but hopefully to bring peace to the individual soul. The private human soul. That will help each man or woman to discover his God.

Now I must contradict myself. There are plenty of people who do love and rejoice in the church, in going to its buildings, serving there, worshiping there. It is a tangible expression of a glorious conviction, it activates God.

Dick Steere—a white-thatched grandfather in our choir whose face has the ebullience of a little boy. Beaming, he marches down the aisle, his voice ringing out in literal paeans of praise. Never mind the time-worn hymns—to him they're just great! And his wife, Francesca, vibrantly present at every service, prayer meeting, study group, retreat. Doing all possible good works and insisting fervently, "What we all need is Jesus Christ in our lives, he is the answer!"

And oh, the countless young couples working together with enthusiasm in the church. And the marriages that have been saved by pastoral counseling and getting back to church . . . Here, too, memories: a particularly stormy, spectacular pair in our little town "saved" at a revival; they went on to become true pillars of our church. Times aren't really so different. Today the church stands better equipped than ever to help heal troubled unions, offers more opportunities than ever for joyous growth through Christ and the company of his people. (Was a stricken marriage ever restored in a night club or country club? I wonder.)

And the women who meet in homes or at the church or on weekend retreats to pray with each other, to share problems, to seek ways to be better wives and mothers, ways to bring children up as good, loving Christlike people in a brutal, self-serving world. And these women, most of them busy women with families—and their husbands, too—joining forces to visit the sick and the elderly, minister to the poor, the lonely, to almost every form of need . . .

My own simple, old-fashioned, dear, sweet, cordial-courteous steepled church on the corner. However tempting it may seem not to go (habit patterns), once I hear the bell clanging and walk in the door, the familiar miracle happens. I'm glad I came! A joy always fills me, a sense of blessing. Okay, so some of the hymns strike me as pretty ridiculous, and I don't always get as much out of every sermon as I should. . . . I can read the Psalms; or I can study the lovely windows or the altar with its beautiful bouquets. And the gold cross says something deeply moving to my heart. And when I go to kneel and receive the sacraments, my agitated spirits are eased. The fragrance of the flowers, the scent of the wine, the delicate flicker of the candles . . . all, all combine to give me a profound sense of the presence of God.

And afterward the fellowship. To talk and drink coffee with kindred spirits. To meet friends like this in a setting that was created for a unique purpose: to worship and if possible serve God. Never mind how far from that purpose we all may have drifted—the church stands for it and tries, it keeps trying. For good.

To draw people together for good. To baptize them and marry them and bury them and comfort them and advise them and introduce them to other people who need each other under a common shelter for good. Almost the first structure built in every settlement in the New World was the church. People had to have it for all these things. In *Virginia, the New Dominion,* Virginius Dabney tells us that even during the agony of Jamestown, the church "provided one of the few centers of social life with its services, weddings and funerals. . . . The Reverend Robert Hunt had held Holy Communion as one of his first acts, following the arrival of the original settlers in 1607."

No—how could any community survive without the church? And though I deplore the lavishness, the utter appalling waste of many churches, even the Lord reminded us, "Man does not live by bread alone." . . . The ancient cathedrals of Europe, built at such severe cost in money and sacrifice. Yet they stand as a serene and moving testimonial to something awesome. The sheer immensity of most of them, Coventry, Westminster, Rheims. The staggering beauty. The genius behind their windows, the pale light, the gentle hush . . . To stand beneath those soaring arches, to kneel on the cold stone floors and pray, surrounded by their effigies, is to feel the soul go thrilling up . . . up to the very throne.

The church is not a building. It is people. But just as we can't raise a family without a place to house them, how can we have a church without a place to gather? This poses a problem. It's so easy to confuse house with *home,* place with *purpose.* Yet it helps to go to the place, the house. The very place can be an inspiration. It needn't be magnificent, it can be small and humble, yet it can be a vital focal point for finding God.

Help Us to Find You There

Lord, please forgive me my ambivalence and confusion about the church. Help me to understand what Christ really meant when he spoke of establishing his church.

All this superstructure that has been imposed upon the simple message preached from a street corner or beside the sea. All these human acquisitions, purely human concerns. Can they be or should they be stripped away? So that the church stands naked and pure and raw, crying salvation to the sinner, ministering to the poor?

Can I or should I try to strip away the vast weight of my own acquisitions, material and mental? So that I, too, stand naked and raw before you, yielded and ready to serve?

The world has changed so much, society has changed so radically. We are no longer a people with a passion for salvation, we are a peo-

ple greedy for more. More comforts, more pleasure, more friends, more fun, more things. More excitement, more sex, more kicks. While our hearts are sick within us, our souls are sick with this surfeit of the things we already have, and the insatiable appetite for more. When what we are really starving for is more YOU.

Lord, help the church find a way to appease that hunger when we come. Ready or not, worthy or not, dutifully or not, scared or not —whatever our motive, we come hoping to find you in your church.

Help us to remember your promise, "Where two or three are gathered together, I'll be there." You are there, Lord, you are there!

Open my eyes to see you, open my ears to hear you, open my heart to receive you. Don't let me miss you in the crowd.

Don't Try to Dissect My Rainbow

Agnes Sanford says: "Religion is an experience of God. Theology is merely an attempt to explain the experience."

Well, who needs it (except the theologians)? What most of us really need is the *experience*. And for me, at least, theology can actually hinder, get between. Theology is like trying to enjoy the rainbow with somebody at your side analyzing it for you. Or it's like thrilling to a poem and then having some teacher tear it apart. Or Robert Frost's "Stopping by Woods on a Snowy Evening," which John Ciardi took five thousand words to explain . . . and Frost's amusement: "Gee, I didn't know I'd meant all that." Critics and theologians can read all sorts of meanings into things even an author never intended.

So I think it must be with God, who must stand back in amazement sometimes at the tons of literature written to "explain" religion to the masses. As if we are too dumb to understand our own experience. Or must be coached to the point of such confusion that we quit before we have it!

No, no, the more some theologians grapple with the direct and yet elusive quality of God, the more obscure and hard to understand they make him. The result—sheer exhausting obstruction. Just compare the language in some of their books to the simple New Testament account of Christ's birth, death, and resurrection. Or take his own words in the Sermon on the Mount. Jesus spoke to men and

women as a man, with a message he wanted them to get. He knew
better than to talk over their heads or try to impress them with his
erudition.

His spokesmen today? Some of them are very good indeed; simple,
direct, honest, emulating that master example as well as any mortal
can. (The church I attend is very lucky in this respect.) But when
they turn away from that example, speak in sonorous pieties, stereo-
types, generalities, abstractions, or sheer harangues, they can actually repel people on their search for God. True, some people would
criticize the Apostle Paul. But in the main most of us slip into the
pew with expectancy, often a wistful hope that this time something
will happen. Some words to excite the imagination, challenge the intellect, throw a fresh light on an old truth. And when this happens we
come back.

True, as one minister I admire and love told me: "You don't go to
church to be *entertained,* you go to worship *God.*" Yet weak, restless
beings that we are, God's spokesmen ought to be able to lead us a
little more deeply into his presence, or at least provide some insight
and strength for the week to come. Many a cynic can be lured into a
church on the sheer strength of the minister's ability, and there, often
to his own surprise, he may find what he only half realized he had
been searching for all along.

Fragment of a Sermon That Helped

"It isn't always a matter of emotion in finding God. We don't feel
him because actually we don't want to. But if we *will* to find him and
practice the ways—church, communion, prayer—the acts themselves will help. . . . 'For lo, I am with you always. . . .' Simply
knowing that and remembering it helps. He *is* with us, whether we
are conscious of it or not. He is seeking us as much as we are seeking
him."

Psychologists tell us "emotion follows action." Will to know him,
practice the ways. . . . Yes, the very act of going to church and worshiping with others keeps me more constant in my will to know God.

Advice from a British Friend

"People who don't send their children to Sunday school 'because
they don't want to go.' You send them to school, don't you? '*Mum, I*

*don't like history.' 'Don't give me that or you'll get the back of me
hand, get outta here!' 'Mum, I can't stand grammar.' 'You can't? Be
off with you, on your way!'* . . . Aaah, parents will abide by the law
and send them to school, but not God's house, not God's school.
They don't want to learn about God? Well, it's your duty to make
them learn about God!"

Four Men of the Ministry

Four men of the ministry who helped make God real for me.

Mr. Howe: Who sometimes supplied our church when I was about
nine or ten years old. I suppose I had a crush on him, very pure and
worshipful. Tall, lean, white-haired. His voice was sweet and soft
and he had a whimsical way; his eyes were deep-set, very blue and
whimsical, too. . . . We didn't kneel in our church, but once when
there was a big feud going on, he actually knelt during the course of
his sermon, and lifting that lean saintly face to heaven, prayed for
the healing of the rift!

I badgered my mother into inviting him to our house for dinner,
and then was so awed by his presence I couldn't eat. He represented
a kind of materialized Christ to me.

Mr. Malone: Young, with a bush of black curly hair and snapping
black eyes and the eloquence of the Angel Gabriel. He preached the
old-time religion with genuine originality and fervor. He dramatized
every story in the Bible, shouting and gesturing as he paced the pulpit. Will I ever forget his Easter sermons as he stood shaking his fist
toward the cross and sneering: "And they taunted him, 'You im-
postor, if you're really the Son of God, save yourself, *come down!'* "

The sweat rolled down his cheeks, and the tears, too, sometimes.
He really stirred us up; poor as we were, he shamed us out of the little white frame building on which bigger, finer churches could look
down. By some miracle we raised the money for a new one, but the
effort split the congregation and broke his heart. "They crucified
him," Mother would say grimly. "They crucified Malone."

Before this happened he took my confession and baptized me,
plunging me deep into the water. I clung to him as I came up, and
maybe if I had been able to cling to him a little longer . . .

Those are the only two ministers I remember from a long procession of them while I was growing up. They made God real to me.

Two more stand out of a lifetime later.

Bob Trenbath: A small dark modest man with curly hair gone white at the temples, and horn-rimmed glasses. He and his family lived in the rectory next door, and the day we moved in he came shyly, bearing a glass of jelly from his wife. In a busy city, to be called on before the trucks were unloaded! And Edith, his wife, was just as nice—blunt, happy-go-lucky, dropping in often for coffee and solemn or uproarious woman-talk. . . .

But Bob. My daughter and I fell promptly in love with him and would rush to the window sometimes just to watch him go past. . . . There was something hauntingly familiar about him—and then I realized, Mr. Howe! That same gentleness, that straightforward twinkling simplicity. His sermons were little gems, delivered in a kind of surprised and wondering manner. (He'd been an engineer before going into the ministry; did that partly explain his tone of freshness and discovery?) And when he read the words for the communion service, "Hear what comfortable words our Lord said—" my own surprised heart *was* comforted. Even knowing my lingering misgivings, he confirmed me in the Episcopal faith. He was a compassionate and very understanding man. To our shock and sorrow, he went on to St. Albans (a part of the Washington Cathedral) and there died suddenly one morning of a heart attack. He was only forty-two.

Ray Ryland: Bob's successor. People marveled—how could we be so lucky? A brilliant and handsome man with a brilliant and beautiful wife, and two small daughters who became playmates of ours. Ray's jubilance in God. His sheer radiance. He strode down the aisle with that procession, beaming as if he'd just found gold. Every statement, read or made in the service, was a kind of "Joy to the world!" . . . Down the street, a wonderful old lady who knew she was going to die. We would see him pedaling past on his bicycle carrying her the sacraments. And he made her so aware of the coming glories she told us (inviting each friend in, by turn, to tell us good-by), "I can hardly wait!"

Ruth and Ray Ryland were, and are, the most exciting, infectious, *total* Christians I have ever known. They live their religion in every word, handclasp, smile, act. Though Ray and I quarreled mightily (and rather enjoyably) over my partial paganism, our friendship went deep, surviving time and distance and many moves. They have made extreme sacrifices for what they believe, and remain radiant people of God, a family of God (six children now). A vigorous and very attractive force for a living God.

How grateful I am for these four men who helped me to know God in the beginning, and later helped give him back to me.

Thank you for them, Lord, and for all the others, seen and unseen along the way. Their voices from radios or TV. Their words in letters and books. Their messages from countless pulpits. Their counsel across a kitchen table.

They have visited me in illness, rushed to my aid in times of trial. They have befriended, encouraged, and comforted me. (And they have put up with me!)

Thank you for every one of them—from the eager young seminarians to the silver-haired substitutes. Thank you for their courage, their kindness, their personal sacrifice, their patience.

They're not perfect, Lord (but neither am I). Help me never to expect of them perfection. And never to confuse the issue so that I begin to make any man of God the object of my worship—even my source of strength—instead of you.

Let me remember always that no man, however inspired or dedicated, can find God for me. He can only help me to find you for myself.

Make a Joyful Noise

Another thing that sometimes gets between me and God in churches is the forlorn music many still use. Hymns more reminiscent of death and anguish than the joyous occasions that knowing and worshiping God should mean. Hymns that date back to the Middle Ages, or at least the long ago.

Once, trying to relieve my boredom, I leafed through the hymnal and read the dates and directions for their rendition with a kind of grim fascination: *1564—With stateliness. 1896—Solemnly. 1773— Slowly, with dignity.* And the words! . . . Clichés of such lugubrious and threatening content I didn't know whether to laugh or cry. Except for a few vigorous and almost gay old favorites, in heaven's name (literally) let's get rid of them. Let's give the go-ahead to bright young writers and musicians who can give us some songs that will make God real to us today!

I don't mean songs of social protest, which merely exploit God, or songs that are flip and sexy, that blaspheme. I simply mean a new music that testifies to the reality and thrill of the search for him; and to the marvelous fulfillment and challenge of the discovery that God is neither dead nor shrouded in antiquity, but very much alive and with us right now. I think there should be a lot more hymns about God's presence on the job and in the kitchen and while running on the beach with a child. About hope and heartbreak and exultation; about a hundred things that are seldom if ever mentioned in church songbooks at all.

They are being composed, but not enough; and they are not used often enough, except for way-out services, or maybe a wedding for way-out people.

Way out. Way *out* . . . The very term should say something to us. People are seeking, sincerely seeking, for a *way out* of the stultifying traps religion itself has kept us in too long. And we must find that way and take it if we hope to help each other find God.

Six Words, Five Men

We ask so much of our churches. Yet Richard Wurmbrand tells how in Russia during Stalin's time there were five men sentenced to die for crimes against the state. All were atheists. But as they realized the end might be near, they began to think about death. And one of them remembered just one phrase his mother had sung when he was small and she rocked him to sleep: "Safe in the hands of Jesus." She had been carried off by the Communists and that is all he remembered of her. Those six words.

He repeated them to the other men, and they began to discuss Jesus. First his hands—his pierced hands. Could those pierced hands now keep them safe? Had those pierced hands really led to resurrection? . . . If so, might there not be resurrection for them? . . . And out of a fragment of song—*six words*—five men found the Lord. Six words, more simple, direct, and profound than volumes of theology.

Be Careful, God Present

Why is it that people who never set foot in a church feel qualified to attack the church so vociferously? . . . That bright young man at the dinner party the other night sounding off with all the hackneyed accusations: The hypocrites and phonies, the people who went "to see and be seen." The empty emphasis on form.

I asked him if he'd been to church lately and he said no, not for years. So how could he possibly know about:

The coffeepot . . . It's already on when you arrive in most churches. Smell that friendly fragrance. Have a cup before services if you want, and afterward as well.

Come as you are . . . Long gone the days when your heart broke if you didn't have a new outfit for Easter. When hats were a must, both to satisfy your vanity and because the tenets decreed. (I'll never forget the day a hatless girl was spotted by one rector, who embarrassed her and everybody else by sending a scarf down to cover her head.) . . . Pants suits at the altar sometimes. A golfer in shirt sleeves. And in the country church just down the road from us a farmer in overalls. (He wasn't being disrespectful, he hadn't had time to change, and the Lord and nobody else cared. The main thing was—he was there!)

Jazz masses. Dance worship. Young people reading modern psalms to a background of their own guitars.

The church where, just before the final hymn, the minister says: "Turn to shake the hand of your neighbor. Now get up and move somewhere else to visit a few minutes with somebody you don't know. . . . Now let's all join hands as we sing—!"

No, if you haven't been to church for a while you may be in for some surprises. You'll just have to start looking for new excuses if you really don't want to go.

But if you do, be careful. You're liable to find God there.

Where Two or Three Are Gathered

One thing sure, you will find God present where even two or three people come together to pray or study the Bible, or even just to discuss him. Some of my happiest, surest moments with God have been seated on the floor in somebody's rec room or on a patio bench or a grassy hillside with others who feel close to him or long to know him better.

The true church is not the institution. It is not the buildings. It is not the place you meet, but *why* you meet. To become more deeply involved with your own Creator and his son, Jesus.

No matter how small the group, he'll be there, too. He promised.

Prayer

*Much keeping company with God will
teach us who God is.*

Charles W. F. Whiston

Open the Door

During my struggles a friend said to me: "Do you find God or does God find you?"

"I don't care, I just want us to find each other!"

"Then open the *door*. . . . What you must realize is—God wants you even more than you want him. He stands at the door knocking. The Bible depicts that image graphically. Your restlessness—it's because you hear that knocking, but refuse to open the door. Maybe you're afraid to, or think you're too busy. And the Lord will keep on knocking . . . but after a while he won't knock so loud or so often, and finally you won't hear it any more, he'll go away."

"*How* do I open the door, what do I do?"

"Talk to him. That's all prayer is. Use prayer."

Yes, of course. . . . How can we know people if we never speak to them? How can we understand people if we never talk to them? If I am ever to get close to God I've got to invite him *in*. No matter how messy my house is, or how frantically much I've got to do. The more often I greet him the more comfortable I feel in his presence, the more he becomes my friend. And the more I talk to him, the more of his nature is revealed to me. "Much keeping company with God," says Charles W. F. Whiston, "will teach us who God is."

We really don't need a place of peace and privacy in which to meet God (ideal as that would be). That's the trouble—we make excuses for not praying, the same way would-be writers make excuses for not writing. "I haven't got time, there's no place where I can be alone to do it." The real writer doesn't wait for the perfect situation, he writes come hell or high water, often in the midst of chaos, with the phone ringing, doors banging, and sometimes a baby across the lap. He or she writes because the creative drive is so intense he can't help it. He's so miserable not writing he's got to write anyway.

The same is true, at least in part, of a genuine urge to pray. Half the time we're praying whether we realize it or not. The heart is crying out, "Help me! O dear God, I can't stand this much longer—" But if I really want to get hold of God again, I can't depend on these spontaneous outbursts, born usually of desperation. I've got to make God a habit, included in all I do. I must stop inventing excuses for not praying and say: Okay, this situation isn't ideal but it isn't going to stop me. I'm just going to pray as best I can, wherever I am. In the kitchen or making the beds or at my desk or in the car.

Maybe I'm making too much of trying to find God. I've got to remember he's also looking for *me*.

Learning to Pray

You know, Lord, how well you know, the years when I didn't pray (or didn't think I prayed). How could I pray to someone whose very existence I doubted? How could I ask for help from a force I spurned?

Yet all the while I was hungering for you, groping to find your hand as I stumbled in the darkness of my needs. . . . "If I could pray," I thought. "If I could only learn to pray."

But I felt foolish when I tried, I felt phony, insincere. My doubts seemed to rise up like a mockery between us. And you knew my follies and my faults all too well. My tongue was inarticulate— it winced to form the words. My own self-scorn made me impotent, dumb.

I would get up from my fumbling so-called prayers with an empty heart, feeling rejected, turned away. (Was there some secret rubric others had discovered? Some key that would make the heavens open, unlock the special doors?)

I was wrong. In a while, maybe from sheer persistence, something began to happen within me. A sense of being accepted, however unworthy. (No—not merely accepted, welcomed, welcomed home!) And the deep excited stirrings of trust in a power I could not see.

Then I went to the formula you gave in the Sermon on the Mount. "Our father who art in heaven—" How kind that seems. "Hallowed be thy name." The gentle beginnings of worship . . .

"Thy kingdom come" (within me). "Thy will be done" (take over my life, I'm not doing so well) "on earth as it is in heaven." (I like

this earth, I don't know about heaven, but it must be a wonderful place).

"Give us this day our daily bread" (just enough for today, Lord, enough time and money and strength to get through this one day) . . . "and forgive us our trespasses as we forgive—" (are my trespasses blocking the road to you? and my lack of forgiveness for those who've hurt me?).

"Lead us not into temptation" (this I don't understand—you couldn't, you wouldn't—just hang on to me when I am tempted, give me the will not to yield). "Deliver us from evil" (yes, yes, that's what I mean—deliverance).

"For thine is the power and the glory forever and ever." (It is, it is, it has to be, and the more often I admit it, express it, the more I know it's true!)

So in this way I began to get deliverance, Lord. The deliverance I sought. From self-doubt, which was so deeply enmeshed with my doubts of you.

And to learn the fundamentals of prayer: worship, submission, acceptance, plea, and then more worship to seal it. And I began to know then as I realize now that worship itself is the key. The magic key. Prayer brings you close when we come not merely seeking help, but because we want to be with you.

Worship Is Like Saying "I Love You"

Worship. What an awesome word. Exciting, vaguely frightening, conjuring up an Old Testament Jehovah . . . Prostrate yourself, bow down, fall to your knees. . . .

Yet Jesus said, "Our Father." . . . I didn't worship my father, although I loved and respected him. (And his *was* the power, if seldom the glory, poor guy, in our home.)

Worship is instinctive, though. We long to worship something.

"Thou shalt have no other gods before me." . . . All right. We won't. But we can't help having a lot of lesser gods along the way; and to worship them is sweet, very sweet. We set them up on pedestals or thrones, these idols. The movie stars of childhood . . . my eighth-grade English teacher . . . that girl my brother fell in love with—"He worships the ground she walks on," Mother said. . . .

Worship is the supreme self-humbling, an intensity of love and adoration that leads to the supreme ecstasy. And God wants us to have it in our relationship to him. This must be why God repeatedly tells us to worship him. Not that he needs it, but *we* need the emotions it creates in us. Worship is like saying "I love you" to the beloved. It reaffirms the shining bond between us. It helps to keep that love alive.

And how can we worship without being grateful? Giving thanks in all our beings for the sheer privilege of being here to witness the marvels of creation—from the magnificence of stars and mountains to the frailest blue harebell or humblest mouse. How can we worship God without rejoicing and being grateful for the greatest marvel of all—self? One's own precious, sentient self, and every circumstance of its life experience.

Gratefulness! Just being grateful—that, too, flings open even wider the door to God. . . . One thing is sure, I can never hang on to God if I keep right on whining and complaining, blaming other people, the world, and sometimes even the weather, for what seems my dismal lot. In essence, blaming God! No, no, such ingratitude is an insult to my Creator. It's like slamming the door on God.

Certainly, I'm human, and plenty of times I'll give vent to my anguish. But when my howls of protest drown out my hosannas, I am bolting the door against his presence, doomed to a self-imposed prison. And when I thank him, ah when I thank him, I have already begun to cancel out the things that trouble me.

So I will praise and thank him and be continually grateful, whether I plan to confront him with a list of problems to be solved or not. And I will certainly thank him when I ask for help.

I will preface each plea with thanks for whatever is already *right*. And thank him for the health and strength and opportunity, with his love, to make things better.

Above all—whether I'm praying by appointment or praying on the run, I will worship and rejoice in his gift of life with its abundance of blessings. This is the quickest way to open the door, this is the surest reunion.

And when my desire to worship outweighs my desire to present my petitions, then I have grown in the art of prayer.

Discoveries in Prayer: A Scattering

. . . Substitute a prayer for worry!

When the mind gets all messy with problems, substitute a prayer. Not a prayer about the problems, but a little song of praise for God himself. It will take your mind off your problems, and in your withdrawal help to solve them, since your worry tensions are not being sent into the atmosphere. . . . (And it gets a lot of praying done!)

. . . For a long time I stopped praying at night, because it just seemed to stir up my worries. Taking inventory of them (even with God) made me so aware of them I couldn't sleep.

I hadn't really turned them over to him, I had actually aggravated them by expressing so much concern. Prayer should never be negative, heavenly hand-wringing. This blocks the way to help and healing.

The power lies always in the affirmative. The positive. Effective prayer seems to come from expectancy, believing.

The Lord must prefer optimists. I don't blame him.

. . . Catherine Marshall speaks of the prayer of relinquishment. There comes a time when you've got to stop badgering God and just trust him to do whatever is necessary and best. Acknowledge your acceptance of his resolution.

No, not merely accept, which smacks of resignation. Actually thank him for it!

. . . Praying about human conflicts, seeming injustices in business or marriage, quarrels and clashes between you and your children or neighbors or friends:

I've learned to ask only that the outcome be truly fair and right. "If *they're* wrong, show them. If I'm wrong, show *me*. Give us all more understanding, and cover this whole situation with love. Move each one of us to do, not merely what our emotions clamor for us to do, or what we feel justified in doing, but what is *right*."

What a relief this is. How it helps to silence the torment of mental machinery—the protests, accusations, rebuttals—as we let wiser, all-seeing forces take over. I can rest assured in the knowledge that sooner or later justice, genuine justice, will prevail.

. . . I've discovered it helps to pray aloud. When prayer is totally thought, the mind is inclined to wander. It drifts from a dialogue with God to plans and programs, an argument, a discussion, something read. Or you'll be asking God's help with a problem and the problem itself takes over: "If Jimmy wouldn't be so stubborn, we've told him that car's not *safe*—"

But if I address myself to God aloud, if I say the words aloud or in a whisper, my own ears keep order. I pay attention, so God can pay attention. This means I do have to find a time and place in which to pray—at least pray comprehensively—and privacy is hard to achieve. But if I really want it, I'll find that time and place. With God nothing is impossible.

. . . An appointed time and place. This does help in coming to grips with God.

Another analogy with writing: To be most productive a writer ought to have a study where he can work regularly at certain hours. Procrastination will stop deviling him; sheer habit will drive him there. Sure he can write if he has to in a bathtub, or with cats and kids crawling all over him; but to produce any serious body of work he must keep definite dates with his calling.

I hadn't realized the importance of this in regard to prayer until Tom Raley, a director of Young Life, shared with me a little booklet by Ben Campbell Johnson, *The Great Discovery*. Filled with invaluable insight and suggestions, it persuaded me to keep even brief appointments with God: Before breakfast, or after getting people out of the house. After lunch. And a longer session at the day's close . . . Three times a *day*? Well, we eat three meals a day, don't we? And the spirit needs nourishment, too.

. . . Make a list of people to pray for. And make a list of things to pray about.

It's so easy to promise to pray for people, or just plan to pray for people, and forget. So many afflictions, so many tragedies or desperate hopes that cry out for intercession. Only an instant of my time, only a few words, a thought—and who knows? It may be the only word of prayer that person will get. . . . Or my prayer will join the chorus of other prayers that often work such miracles.

And prayers for others *always* help, if only the one who prays. That isn't my motive in praying for them, no, but it's legitimate to remember: It's impossible to pray for someone else without being

strengthened yourself. Why? I don't know, except it's one of those
undeniable laws: Give, even so much as a prayer, a thought, and
you receive.

But I'm so busy, so preoccupied with my own affairs. The reg-
ulars—these of course I remember—but the others I forget unless
I write them down. So keep the notebook handy, add their names
to my list. . . .

It's a fine thing, too (if you can find the time and make yourself
do it), to list the other things you need to pray about. Personal faults,
like jealousy or self-pity. Concerns about a husband's job (or your
own) or the children's grades. Even something as seemingly trivial
as a date for your daughter or a new sofa in time to entertain. These,
as well as the great soul-wrenching issues . . . set them down if you
can, and look back on the list a few months or years later.

It's a great way to measure your progress as a person. And to
restore your faith in prayer . . . All those things you were worry-
ing about! Half of them didn't happen. The rest were resolved or
have simply gone away. . . . Eva Light, a friend at church. Able to
laugh as she recalled the horrors the family went through when
"every single child had become a hippie. We didn't think a one of
them would turn out to be a civilized citizen. Now they're all happily
married or Ph.D.s!"

True, there is a dependable set of new concerns to take their
place. (My mother used to say, "You never get rid of your problems,
you simply exchange them for others.") But written evidence of
the passing of what once seemed so critical gives us courage to face
the present and is strong witness to the power of prayer. . . .

Wait here—slight correction. . . . Some problems may never quite
go away. We get used to seeing them on our lists of life (real or
rhetorical), used to living with them. . . . Prayer-eradicated? No—
but at least prayer-assuaged. And everybody has his "bundle." This
just may be mine to bear.

. . . "When you talk to God, aren't you really talking to yourself?"
a TV commentator once asked me.

I told him, "Sure."

"Then how do you know the answers aren't simply coming from
yourself?"

"I don't," I said. "God made me. He is in me. He is the greater, wiser part of myself watching over me. Calling on God is also calling on this greater self. That's why prayer can be counted on to help. God isn't off someplace tuning me in from a star. He's in me, right here."

"Don't you wish he'd answer aloud sometimes? How do you know he's listening if you can't hear him?"

"Can't *hear* him? Listen—to the mother of a big noisy family that's great! A God who answers in silence is what most of us prefer."

. . . *Bless.* What a beautiful word. Lively and musical and full of joy. And holding within itself one of prayer's dearest secrets. For the happiest prayers of all are when we call down blessings on people. Send a blessing winging their way for no good reason except a sudden desire to wish them well.

Compassion stirs the heart to bless. . . . Two old people waiting anxiously on the wrong side of the street for a bus that doesn't come. I will cross the street to help them, yes, but more—I will ask God to bless them when they climb safely aboard. . . . A little boy whose mother is shaking and slapping him mercilessly in a store. "Dear God, restrain her, love her, bless her . . . and oh please help and bless that little boy." . . . A figure crouched on deserted steps at midnight, his face in his hands. Far below my hotel window— there is no way I can reach out to touch him, help him—all I can do is ask God to touch him, bless him. . . .

If you hurt for other people, sometimes a blessing is the only way you can comfort yourself. . . . And if you rejoice for other people, blessing enhances your own happiness. . . . A neighbor's daughter receives the school's highest award. Hooray for her and for her family—bless her, bless them all! . . . An old friend who's struggled for years finally sees his dream come true. Bless him. . . . The runaway child is home again . . . the operation is over (it wasn't cancer, after all) . . . the estranged couple is reunited . . . the disaster, financial or otherwise, is averted for people you care about—or even people you don't know well. I will thank God as fervently for them as I would for myself. I will bless them. . . .

How can I ever be jealous or envious of anyone, God, so long as I remember to bless them?

How can I want to hurt or wish ill to a single living soul?

Blessing activates my compassion. Blessing is personal consolation when I am powerless to do more.

A blessing takes no time, costs nothing. Yet it warms the heart, puts a smile on the face and a lilt in the spirit. How can I be unhappy, at least for long, when I use this dear yet simple word, "bless"?

. . . Jesus promised that God will answer our prayers if we ask in his name and believe.

But he gives only what is best for us (and others), and what we are ready, truly ready to receive.

I can look back on my life and see so many places where I wanted to settle for less, so much less. And got mad at God when the thing I begged for didn't happen . . . unable to comprehend that he might be biding his time. Waiting for other people to be ready. Waiting for *me* to be ready to accept, and handle, the greater blessings he had in store.

You can't hold a stop watch on God. You can't confine him to a calendar. God's time is not our time. And he often has greater plans for us than we can possibly conceive.

. . . Prayer has to be me. My own personal business with God that nobody else can arrange for me. But in prayer, as in anything else, we can learn from each other.

I like to vary the patterns of prayer. Praying about the same things in the same order all the time may keep you from floundering, but you can also fall into a rut, lose the sense of renewal that comes with spontaneity. And you don't always have to pray in the same place. Pray at the window, pray outdoors. Take the dog for a run under the stars and pray on the way. Pray on the porch or in the garden.

Don't feel guilty about the times when you just don't want to pray—when you even come to God grudgingly. A curious thing happens, once you begin to thank him and tally up your blessings (in spite of!), peace and pleasure pour in. Some of the times when I really dreaded praying proved to be the longest, most rewarding sessions. Almost—well, almost like making a duty call, and having such a wonderful time I didn't want to leave.

. . . The more often we pray, the better we get at it. Or maybe not "better." Just more comfortable, more confident and clear. We realize God doesn't demand any special ritual or fancy phrases; he doesn't mind if we're awkward. But prayer is spiritual exercise. And the more often we pray, the more graceful (full of grace?) we will be. But stronger, that's the main thing, the stronger we grow in our relationship to God.

To Summarize the Day

I seldom wake up in the morning without a little start of pleasure just at being here, alive and ready for another day. . . . The good night's sleep behind me (too good sometimes—the warm bed urges, "Come back!"). *Thank you, God.* . . . Or even a night broken by too many dreams and a brain that refused to quit . . .

At least my body rested, and maybe my brain needed that silent time to think—so thank you, God. . . .

The feel of feet on the floor, flesh responding to the comfort and bite of hot and cold water in the shower. The smell of breakfast cooking, the ability to *get* breakfast, hear people coming, laugh, listen, scold, speak . . .

The miracle of water and food and human contact—who am I to deserve all this? Thank you, thank you!

And the bright day ahead, so full of promise and challenge and work to be done, problems to be solved, things to be overcome, yet each hour an adventure, each minute a mystery. That I should be here at all . . . that I should be so lucky as to have this day. Even one day! (If each soul could have only one day on earth and knew it in advance, souls would be lined up for blocks wherever souls are, awaiting their turns.)

Thus the day's first prayers. Relate your awareness of your own existence to your gratefulness for it, and you've got a prayer.

At night I come to God more leisurely. Something makes me want to draw it all together, summarize it with its Creator. Look it over to see where it fits in the pattern of my life. To rejoice over what went right, puzzle over what went wrong, and ask his guidance for tomorrow.

And to lay my problems out in some more orderly fashion than the hectic, piecemeal way in which they've been flung at him all day. To seek insight to understand them better, and the knowledge to solve them, or even just the strength to *endure* them.

And at this end of day I want to gather up all the people I care about and ask for help for them. Those who are in trouble, those who need healing. I'm so busy and the list is long . . . if I don't keep this standing appointment with God, I might not do it.

And to pray for the people who've gone on. To ask the Lord to bless them, convey my continuing love to them . . . I never used to see the slightest sense in praying for the "dead." But now that I know they have only advanced to a different degree of living, how can I neglect them? And there is joy and comfort in relating to them at least once a day.

And to ask the Lord to bless this just-lived day. Take it under consideration and use it to some good purpose in the scheme of my own life and the many lives it has touched. . . . Did I hurt anyone today? Did I help someone? Did this one day of my life have an effect, an influence on others?

And the effect of others on me . . . Did someone hurt me? Bless that person and help me to forgive. (Or even profit by what was done or said.) . . . And the people who helped me, made me happy —don't let me forget them, even if it's only in a flood of rejoicing and thanksgiving as I remember. . . .

Oh, there are so many lives mingling and overlapping in the course of a single day. Even if we don't see people—through letters, phone calls, thoughts, or something that may be happening unknown to us far away—yet the living threads entwine. And for most of us, busy, surrounded by others, it is amazing even to consider the constant interweaving of lives that causes so many things to happen to us in even one average, prosaic day.

So there's lots to consider and reflect on when it comes to the final prayer of the day. Yet the prayer needn't be long. Its scope can be immense and yet compressed in a small segment of time. . . . Such a peaceful, shining, strength-renewing time, this prayer to summarize my life this day.

Thank you, Lord, that the door between us is never closed. That I finally learned to open that door to you.

The Arts

*Build thee more stately mansions, O
my soul!*

Oliver Wendell Holmes

More Stately Mansions

"Build thee more stately mansions, O my soul!"—Another of Mother's favorite quotations. From *The Chambered Nautilus,* by Oliver Wendell Homes . . . She looks up from the washboard with a twinkle in her eyes, tosses back a lock of her long dark hair, and goes on, as her hands wring out the clothes: "As the swift seasons roll! Leave thy low-vaulted past!"

Oh, Mom, that little house where you worked so hard! . . . You could have held your own in any stately mansion, and you set foot in so few during your life. But then why should you? you already occupied so many. Mansions of the spirit, mansions of the mind. The Lord had given you the keys, and you wandered them at will. . . . Through books—of poetry, especially. Through the music you listened to with such pleasure ironing, baking, keeping your family clean. Through copies of famous paintings cut so carefully from magazines.

It was years before you saw the originals of some of those paintings in the galleries. How awed and astonished you were at their size. A gigantic Rubens, I remember, claiming half a wall—though it had hung cozily in its dime-store frame over your bed and Dad's for years. You gasp, then giggle behind your hand—"Suppose Rubens ever dreamed he'd hang in *our* stately mansion?"

Stately mansions . . . the cold marble floors ring beneath our heels as we walk them, Mother and I, under the vaulted ceilings. The flowers are bright in the courtyards, the fountains sing and splash. We wander from picture to picture, sitting often to rest, for she's getting old now and her feet hurt and she has to get her breath. . . . We sit loving the place, its sculpture, its brasses and bronzes and tiles. Then we rise and find the oriental wing. . . . How she loves the Chinese porcelains. Getting her big round reading glass from her bag, she studies each huge vase or urn carefully, remarking the exquisite detail, the intricacy of design. And now she alludes to "Kubla Khan": " 'Through wood and dale the sacred river ran, Then reached the caverns measureless to man.' You know I'd have loved to have a Ming vase, but unfortunately the Jewel Tea man never gave them for premiums, and I doubt if you could get one today with trading stamps."

Even as I laugh and hug her, my heart breaks. I want, with sudden blind passion, to place her in her stately mansion surrounded by all the beautiful things her soul craves.

But later, long after she's asleep, I go outside and gaze up at the stars sparkling so brightly. And the last few lines of her *Chambered Nautilus* come to me:

> Let each new temple, nobler than the last,
> Shut thee from heaven with a dome more vast,
> Till thou at length art free,
> Leaving thine outgrown shell by life's unresting sea!

And then the words, from another source altogether: "In my Father's house are many mansions."

Mother will have her mansions.

Water into Wine

In Jane Robinson's book *Edward G. Robinson's World of Art* the famous actor-collector is quoted: ". . . If man could make this beauty on my walls, if he could produce the life and form and color that make the magic of these canvases, and do it only from tinted earth, stirred with insight and passion and faith, why then, there is hope for us all."

Hope for us all. For me not only hope, but evidence of God. For like music, painting is a mystery and a magic. How is it that anyone can sit, crayon in hand, and swiftly sketch the likeness of another man, woman, or child? Not only the outline of the head, the shape of the body, but the special expression of lips and eyes and tilt of chin that declares this is Jane or Russ or Pat or Judy and no one else? How is it that the portrait painter, using only a brush dipped in colored oils, can reproduce on a flat square of cloth or board an individual so alive he almost speaks? And in the process draw forth from face, figure, stance and expression the deep secrets of character nobody else has seen or may even suspect?

How is it that a Corot or a Constable or a Gauguin can go into the forest, set up his easel, and return at night with an entire landscape captured, so that years later people standing before the finished product can almost hear the waterfall, smell the ferns, and feel the warm sunshine as it spills across the trees? Or a Winslow Homer can send the sea thundering between the confines of a frame? Or a Käthe Kollwitz, with a few strokes of a thick black pencil, can re-create forever the agony of a mother in Nazi Germany passionately protecting her child?

Yes, there are technics, devices, skills, to be learned. But first, before they can be taught, there must be the fierce bright gift within. I was lucky enough to be in college with Herbert Rosengren. He'd come back to finish and teach our water-color class. Some of us had it and some of us didn't, and though he was always kind he made that clear. Nobody could ever make an artist out of anyone who lacked that special gift.

One of his own works was a sculptured head of Christ. Bowed, so simple and profoundly beautiful and alive, it made me gasp. "How do you do it, Herb?"

"Who knows? It's magic, Marj."

Years later, after he'd become famous, we met again and again discussed the eternal mystery of art. And his answer was just as short and direct as before. "There is no explaining it. It's magic, Marj."

He didn't think he believed in anything, and he kidded me about God. Yet magic/miracle—what is the difference? Who planted that special flame within that enlivened his vision and activated his hands? The artist who can transform paint and stone and wood and steel into tears and trees and human emotions—does he not share the nature of Christ who walked the waves and caused the blind to see? Doesn't he, too, turn water into wine?

The Master

How can I stand before the work of any of the masters and not think of the Master?

That day at the National Gallery in Washington . . . What wing was I in—Spanish? Byzantine? . . . Anyway, all these likenesses of the Holy Family, and the crucifixions . . . And one, where they were taking down Jesus' battered body from the cross. Who painted it? I don't remember. Only that it caught me and would not let me go.

I was in a hurry, about to leave, and yet it held me, and I suddenly wanted to cry. . . . That face, so silent after suffering. Those bruises, wounds beginning to swell. But more—one of the women— Mary? was bending forward to cover his naked thighs where the cloth was slipping. . . . And the awful *humanity* of it tore me, for I realized that this man was real.

He was flesh and blood and bone. He had hair on his chest and on his limbs, and his mother hastened to cover his nakedness.

Suddenly, overpoweringly, an artist had given me God.

The "Pietà"

Stone is so mute. Hard, impenetrable. Seemingly lifeless. But stone in the hands of an artist! . . .

Michelangelo. The "Pietà." The only work, they say, he ever signed. On a band across the Virgin's tunic: MICHAEL-ANGELUS-BONAROTUS-FLORENT-(INUS)-FACIEBAT (Michelangelo Buonarroti of Florence made this) . . .

Was this the only time he ever felt sufficient pride in his work? This genius who carved the great "David" and painted the story of creation in the Sistine Chapel, including God? Was he always striving, striving for the ultimate? And then, in the moment of sudden awareness when he *knew* . . . knew he had achieved it and nothing could surpass this creation, in love and wonder he scrawled his name.

These fluid bodies, the supreme restraint of Mary's anguish as she holds the prone body of her son. His head fallen back, his hands loose at his sides . . . "It is finished."

Herb, my artist friend, wrote of it in a letter: "Never has stone been turned to flesh in such a marvelous way. The body of Christ is absolutely limp, the robes of Mary a fantasy of convolutions (like the membranes of the uterus of the Universe), and the face of Mary is the mother of the world. What genius, what a biologist, what a physiologist, what an artist! He knew more than he could possibly understand."

An artist does know "more than he can possibly understand." God has chosen him to know, with a blind but sure soul-knowledge. And to express things beyond his own comprehension. Things of God. An artist is but the tool in God's hand.

The Beauty of God, the Lover

Where does the urge to create beauty begin?

Deep in somebody's heart. An itch, an urge, a passion, often love-inspired . . . The child laboring over a surprise for his mother—a lumpy clay elephant, a drawing. That necklace I once made for an aunt—out of pieces of macaroni and an assortment of pearls, beads, and buttons. The rapture of seeing it materialize, convinced it was the most beautiful piece of jewelry in the world.

Or the mother sewing for her child. Why not just simple, sensible garments, especially for a baby who won't know the difference? . . . The Harvest Festival in Irvine, Scotland, at a lovely auld kirk. The minister, in his quaint-seeming robes, perched high in his flower-decked loft. The whole altar was banked with a vivid treasury of offerings and the children marched down the aisle carrying more: sheaves of golden wheat, pumpkins, baskets of bright fruit, home-canned jellies. A mighty outpouring of colorful provender to share with the poor.

And the minister took his text from Psalm 90: "Let the beauty of the Lord our God be upon us." And he said: "Beauty throbs at the heart of living things. Feeling the sunshine on one's face, seeing the ripening grain, we sense this—all nature declares this beauty.

"Some forms of beauty can be attributed to necessity—the color and fragrance of flowers attract the bees for fertilization. But this does not account for the beauty of landscapes, or the lovely forms of trees and clouds. And the theory collapses when we consider the forms of beauty unseen—minute sea creatures, for instance, so exquisite that microscopically examined they rival a rose window in a Gothic cathedral. Biological necessity does not explain.

"Or that young mother picking with a delicate touch the threads of her baby's garment. Putting in a rosebud here, a spray of heather there. Why? Will her baby know how beautiful this tiny garment is? Will it care so long as it is fed and warm? Then why do it? Because the mother is a lover—she cannot help creating beauty.

"God is a god of beauty because he is a god of love. I look at the world as the psalmist did—everywhere the beauty of God, of a lover. 'Never wouldst thou have created anything if thou hadst hated it.' " . . .

Another ancient church, this one in Middleton, England, the Shropshire district, near the Welsh border. Adorned with the carvings of Waldegrave Brewster, a young Welsh clergyman who came to it in 1872. Working primarily by candlelight after his day's duties were done, he glorified nearly every wooden inch of his church— altar, baptismal font, choir loft, columns and pews—and kept a loving logbook of his progress. Knights, angels, a pixie-eared devil in chains; the legend of the kind fairy who told the locals during a hard year they could milk her cow daily, only a wicked witch tried to foil them and was imprisoned in stone for her trouble . . . Even his dogs and his parishioners are immortalized at the ends of the pews—an old lady in a mobcap, a stern bearded elder, a jolly man with a bulbous nose. . . .

Such joy as he must have had in those solitary hours with knife and chisel in hand, such communion as he must have had with the one who gave him such skill. He was worshiping with his fingers.

An artist once said to me: "To be born with a talent is to be born with a curse as well as a blessing. The awful need to do it, and the agony when you keep putting it off, don't do it. And the terrible times when you try, but don't live up to your own expectations, when you fail. But when you get it, when you're doing it and you know it's right, if only for you—but especially when it's right for other people, too, then there's no ecstasy like it. It's like grabbing God's hand for a minute, he's shown you how it feels to be the Creator."

Thank you for this thrill of creating, Lord. For planting this passion to express beauty in so many people.

Your love put it there. Just as you loved us enough to make this world so beautiful for us, you gave us the desire to make it more beautiful still. Thank you for all artists, great and small.

They teach me a lot about you.

Music

Let me try to imagine a world without music. What if you'd given us such a world, God?

Not a silent world necessarily. Let it have the usual noises—sound of voices, pound of feet, bark of dogs . . . roar of engines, click of dishes and pans . . . bang of hammers and typewriter keys and doors. A busy, efficient world but a world without song . . . I can't bear it, the very concept is sad!

Not even bird song? No, this world empty of music would have to forgo even the belling and trilling of birds; only those with raucous cries could remain. . . . Not even a human whistler? No, because it's hard to whistle even at a girl without musical notes creeping in. Factory whistles, yes, calling people to work. Police whistles, traffic whistles, sirens—whistles for duty and danger. Shrill mechanical whistles—but no human whistles because when a person whistles he or she is glad.

And gladness would have little place in a world bereft of music. We would survive, I suppose. We would eat and sleep and work and mate and die. But would we love? Would we rejoice? Would we grieve? Would we be moved to acts of heroism or even acts of kindness? Would we achieve? . . . How could we? Why should we? For music is such an emotional thing. And doesn't everything in life circle round and round and in and out of us in rhythmic patterns of emotion?

Music stirs us, inspires us, uplifts our spirits or depresses them sometimes. ("Turn that off, it's too sad, I can't stand it!") Music charges our energies, our loyalties, our sense of pride—in a nation or a football team. (The flag is flying, here they come, listen to the band!) Music is "the food of love." We flirt to music, fall in love to music, dance, dream, and marry to music. From the lullabies sung at the cradle, to the taps that hurt so terribly, yet somehow make it all seem so right at the grave, music is inextricably entangled with our emotions. An outward expression of things we feel so deeply yet can't articulate.

How can anything so exquisite, so beautiful and powerful come from any source except the mysterious source of us all?

Come on somebody, show me. Dig up some proof, evolutionist; present me with some fact that will explain music. When and where in the meticulous selectivity of the species did music first begin? What manner of man first felt song stirring in his heart? Who or what put that yearning there and why? Who gave him the skill to express it? And where do the melodies come from?

Why the infinite variations, multiple as the stars, so that if you composed for a million years you could never exhaust the supply? . . .

But no, there's no use trying to grasp the why and how of music, it is the most elusive art of all. A painting or piece of sculpture can be felt and touched. A book you can hold in your hand and read. But music?

Listen! . . . It comes to you across the hill, someone singing and playing. . . . It pours through your house from unseen sources (too many sometimes). . . . It may seem visible to you as the violinist moves his bow, the tympanist beats his drums, yet they are only the instruments; shut your eyes and you hear it in all its glory still. Even when you look at the score, you see only diagrams that the musician translates into these marvelous sounds. Sounds that somebody else first heard in his head . . . How come? Why did he hear them in the first place, and from where? And why, once these silent "sounds" have been set down on paper (and who can explain *that* transition?) and transposed by voice or instrument into what we call music, why should these sounds have any effect on *me?*

No, no, the mystery is too much. I give up, I can find no other source for it but God. No other *reason.* God must have given us music to sweeten life with its burdens, to give us an extra dimension for sharing life's emotions. Otherwise what *good* is it? And if it is good, then it is of God.

There must have been music before creation. (The music of the spheres.) There must have been music at the dawn of creation. And when man woke up and found himself upon the earth, I believe he must have heard the birds already singing and uttered his first song. And instinctively he must have reached out for a reed or stick with which to fashion an instrument to enhance and enlarge that song; to express greater feelings than his whistling lips or limited throat could.

The Bible is full of singing and playing . . . of lutes and timbrels and tabrets, of drums and flutes and harps and lyres. "The Jewish nation was a nation of musicians," says Henri Daniel-Rops. They must have music. Music to celebrate harvests and victories and feasts and weddings, music to mourn the dead. And to worship, ah, to worship! . . . David and his psalms. He could never have written those immortal words without the music that accompanied them, and he sang them to both Jehovah and King Saul. . . . The songs of Solomon could only have been born to music, and how much richer our heritage would be if we could know their original tunes. Music pulsates through the whole marvelous, fantastic story of man, civilized and otherwise. Pagan, Jew or Christian, Moslem, Buddhist, Hindu, or American Indian, whatever the religion, music enables mortals to call out to the heavens from which we come. To make contact with our Creator. Music is the bridge sublime.

Isn't it significant that angels sang to announce the birth of Christ? "And suddenly with the angel there was a great throng of the heavenly host, praising God and singing: 'Glory to God in the highest heaven, and peace to men . . .'" (Luke 2:13–14, Jerusalem Bible). God himself turns to music. How else announce that tremendous event? Music, the universal language.

Music throughout the world. No words are needed when great music is played, no translators necessary. Attend an international youth orchestra festival. So many young people from so many countries, different in speech and face and dress. Yet when the conductor lifts his baton and the hands, black or white or brown, lift their instruments, all become as one. And when the strong sweet sounds begin to pour forth, all barriers vanish, the entire assemblage becomes as one. As one they hear and understand this common celestial tongue.

Who or what but an all-powerful common father could be back of such a phenomenon? This, too, a baptism of the Spirit . . .

To be able to hear music, what a blessing. But even the deaf don't miss it altogether. They, too, "hear" the pulsations, feel the rhythms, beat time, often dance. At Gallaudet, famous Washington college for the deaf, they have a robed choir and "sing" with their fingers! . . . The genius of Beethoven, overcoming even the deafness that began at thirty and was total by the time he was forty-nine. Imagine: to hear some of your own masterpieces only faintly, and that great oratorio *Missa Solemnis* not at all. Except in your mind . . .

Except in the mind . . . The miracle of the mind. What is mind but the unseen stuff of God? The ephemeral but potent dust of all creation drifting through our consciousness? Caught, held, transformed into ideas that are in turn transformed into things. Sometimes tangible things like houses and books and colleges and banks and cars. Sometimes that magnificent intangible, music.

How I'd love to be a composer, listening, ever listening for the sound of pianos and strings and brasses in my head, and when I heard them, able to set them down. I know it's not all that easy—but even to wrestle with the sounds, changing and rearranging until I had them meshed into near-perfection. How I'd love even to be a musician, drawing the music from a piano or horn or cello. . . . Observe musicians as they play. They are lost to us, they dwell in another world. They are transported to places where we cannot follow. They are close to the heart of God.

As for us who sit listening . . . we are given glimpses of the divine. For a little while our own world changes, too, its harsh edges soften, melt into something lovely; the darks and the grays brighten, take on living colors; the grim gives way to something that shines. We are soothed or enlivened, delighted or profoundly moved. We forget, we forgive, we want to dance and laugh and love and cry.

Nobody can tell me this isn't your doing, God. Your very breath and being entering ours. Speaking to us, calling to us, using music to stir us, comfort us, uplift us. And giving us a foretaste of even more beautiful music to come.

Poetry

Poetry . . . its rhythms that echo the rhythms of the universe. This, too, speaks to me of God.

In the beginning, the very beginning, a mother rocking her child to sleep—the songs she croons to him, the little nonsense chantings. All this cradling and loving—there is heartbeat back of it all—her own heartbeat and the great heartbeat of God.

With some of us, once this rhythm begins it never ceases; from Mother Goose to Masefield, we respond. From the little gooseboy wandering "upstairs and downstairs, and in my lady's chamber" to Masefield going "down to the sea in ships . . ." And the sea itself rolls in, the waves never varying their patterns. The very wind cries in cadences, and the trees turn into lovely swaying poems in the wind. While the rain pounds out its measures on the roof.

God puts a hunger in some hearts when we are very small; God puts a pencil in the hand. There is no appeasing that hunger unless the pencil moves, too, struggling with these elusive rhythms.

God, and a good librarian, led me to poetry in the wonderful library we had in Storm Lake, my little home town. The poetry books were few, but their treasures overwhelming. Here it had happened, the miracle had happened—the words had been shaped to their delicate true purpose, people had captured the wind!

God led me to the Psalms. . . . I remember almost the very moment as a child in church one morning. The responsive reading. From the pulpit a voice leading: "Thou crownest the year with thy goodness; and thy paths drop fatness." And we, all of us, even those new to the wonder of words, could reply: "They drop upon the pastures of the wilderness: and the little hills rejoice on every side."

The little hills! . . . And the rest: "The pastures are clothed with flocks; the valleys also are covered over with corn; they shout for joy, they also sing."

Something shouted for joy within me, too; the Holy Spirit roused me through this poem. . . . And today, reading the Psalms today, whatever our age, we walk again on hillsides clothed with flocks and corn, and love God and challenge God and bow down before the mystery and the marvel of his never-ending plan.

For the universe, the whole universe, is one great poem. Day and night, birth and death, winter and spring, blossoming and withering, sunshine and storm . . . the metronome swings, the very stars in their courses have such meter they could be scanned.

And even when God himself seems to have gotten lost somewhere, or we have wandered off like the little boy in Mother Goose and can't be found—we have not been banished, and there is no banishing the patterns. The language of the world is never stilled, the great eternal system with its tireless heart pounds on.

And so poetry is of God. True poetry that makes one's own heart leap in recognition. Reading it, poetry that some other tormented or rhythm-rejoicing soul has brought into being, is sometimes as if God himself has struck us down unaware from the printed page.

Yes, oh yes—this is another way to be hurled straight into the heart of God.

His Very World Dances

To me, no art form speaks more eloquently of my Creator than the dance. His very world dances! Almost everything in nature that he has made.

Look out the window, now, right now. Whatever the season, look out upon the vast living stage of the world. How hard it is for nature to be still; even on the stillest summer days the squirrels leap and scurry, the streams cavort, ballets of tiny butterflies dip and swirl. And when the wind stirs——! Even now, November—a chill bright golden day. The grass has nearly lost its green, the trees are almost bare. Yet lean and stripped, those trees lift their arms to the sky as if in worship, and dance. The few remaining leaves do a happy roundelay as they come skirling down. They are little girls in dancing class, skittering this way and that. They skip across my window as I write, land briefly, pirouette on.

Below is the water, sequin-skirted in the sun. Moving, ever-moving to the cadences of its currents and the wind. The waves keep time. Like a perfectly trained chorus, a line of them swings forward arm in arm, white-plumed; bowing their heads in unison they break, rise, surge shoreward, regroup. There with another little bow they disperse, reach toward me, then retreat to dance again.

Soon winter will stop their performance, polish the stage. But then the snows will come dancing down, weaving and twining like Maypole streamers as they fall. . . . Then spring and the triumphal melting, the dancing of rain, the dance of buds on the boughs and petals on the breeze.

Lord, how you must love dancing to put its rhythms into all these things. And into your creatures—insect, bird or beast. To equip them with such grace.

No animal moves clumsily, not even a rhinoceros. Watch them in the wild, watch a herd of elephants—their enormous bodies move in sinuous flow. . . . And *pad-pad-pad* the jungle cats . . . And the agile beauty of monkeys swaying, somersaulting, dancing ceaselessly in their cage. And the gliding curves of reptiles . . . All, all performing their innate patterns. And at mating season many species execute elaborate courting dances.

Man is the only creature who becomes awkward. Why? How strange, since he begins like others with such grace. A baby is superbly graceful—watch the kicking feet, the rhythmic flailing of the tiny star-shaped hands. A child even falls with grace, a kind of liquid collapsing, as if he is in mysterious harmony with the tides and pulses of the universe. Maybe that's why, though he may cry, he's seldom really hurt. And even the merest toddler cannot resist music, he must begin to wriggle and bounce and prance around, trying to dance.

It's when we get older that we become self-conscious, stiffen, hold back this native impulse to express our kinship with all creation. Afraid of how we'll look, of what people might think. Yet when we are excited, filled with delight, we can't help it—we leap for joy, we dance! And when we can let ourselves go, embrace the art and delight of dancing, then we have broken through shackles that would deny and reject a bounty God-bestowed.

People in Bible times were less repressed. Dancing was to them as natural as breathing. They danced at grape treadings and on the threshing floor. They danced at festivals and feasts and to welcome men home from battle. Dancing was a form of worship; they danced at their altars. The very prophets danced as proof of "feeling the hand of God upon them." And so great was David's ecstasy at the return of the Ark he could express it in no other way—he threw off his clothes, except for a linen girdle, "And David danced before the Lord with all his might" (II Sam. 6:14).

Dancing wrong? Sinful? Then the very trees must be sinful, and the water that dances at my feet. . . . No, surely this body, temple of my spirit, is every bit as free and wonderful as that water or a tree. It won't last as long as the ocean or the tree I see swaying before me right now, but it has even more marvelous and varied things to express.

Especially my sheer joy, Lord, in being alive, and my gratefulness to you for allowing me to be.

Nama Lathe, my tiny spinster art teacher in college. I wanted to paint, she said, "Forget it." I wanted to work in clay, she said, "Absurd." I wanted to draw, she said, "Maybe." I could not please her; we were *not* simpatico. But one thing she said impelled me to scrape up the money to attend my first professional dance concert: "I have never had a deeper religious experience than when watching those dervishes." She was right, neither had I.

Since then I have sat enthralled before countless dance companies. Spent hundreds of hours in studios while my own daughters trained . . . Those slender bodies, like a chain of paper dolls. The hard work, the dedication . . . jeté, jeté, glissade, assemblé . . . The toes curl, the whole body yearns; like a child I simply can't hear music without dancing, if only in spirit, in my mind. And I am never closer to the architect of this body "so fearfully and wonderfully made" than when dancing, if only by myself at home.

Dancing, that played such a vital role in religion from the beginning of time. So natural, primitive, direct, expressing childlike faith and joy. How sad that churches, like people, grew up and like people *tightened* up, becoming conservative, civilized, self-conscious, apprehensive of dancing. Now we are beginning to realize our loss. Little by little we find dancing returning to the church, not simply as entertainment but as a legitimate part of the service. Dancers interpreting the litany, adding a lovely visual dimension to the hymns and psalms.

As for me, whether in the church or in my kitchen . . . at the Kennedy Center or my own back yard, the beauty and wonder of dancing—God's whole wonderful world of dancing—makes my heart rejoice, my very soul reach out toward the glory that is God.

The Meeting in the Mansions

"Build thee more stately mansions, O my soul!" I think of that so often, Mother. In a cathedral. Before a great painting. Watching a ballet. Hearing a magnificent voice in song. Listening to an orchestra tuning up, then bursting into the triumphant strains of Beethoven or Mendelssohn or Brahms . . . Not nearly often enough. Perhaps that's why, when I bestir myself to set forth, often at great effort, to take this beauty for myself, the phrase cries out with such urgency and meaning. . . .

All the grubby little houses we settle for in life. The mindless world of game shows, soap opera, Bingo, comic books, slot machines, gambling casinos, of poker and night clubs and cocktail parties. All the cheap and tawdry junk that passes for pleasure—when there are mansions to be explored.

My God, dear God, you have endowed this earth with so much beauty. Laced it, showered it, enriched it with so much that is lovely and enchanting, why do we huddle in our miserable little houses? Why do we settle for the trite, the dull, the ugly, when you have given us the keys to so many mansions?

Poetry and painting, music and sculpture and dancing. Thank you for all these mansions we can enter right here on earth and find you waiting. If I really want to know you better, I have only to open their doors!

Pain

Out of the depths have I cried unto thee,
O Lord. Lord, hear my voice: let thine ears
be attentive to the voice of my supplications.

Psalm 130:1–2

The Choice

I must tackle the subject of suffering, God. I must wrestle with the problem of finding you and not letting go in spite of the awful injustices of your world, in spite of pain.

You know I don't understand it—I don't think many people do, no matter what they claim. I sometimes feel very stupid. Again and again it is explained to me, the purpose and need of suffering. And I listen and nod and agree.

Then I see people who've lived lives of great goodness and sacrifice die sudden dreadful deaths; or trembling through long lonely living deaths in nursing homes. . . . I see the horrible ravages of famine and wars. . . . And the children—O dear God, the little children neglected, abused, raped. Or born crippled, mute, blind.

And my very soul rages. I don't BLAME *you, but there is no sure heart-knowledge of mercy or justice within me. I can only accept the fact (and ask you to forgive me) that I can't accept some things.*

I can only trust to such sure heart-knowledge as I have: That suffering does not come from you. But it is not in vain. It DOES *serve some purpose in the total scheme of things. And you expect us to take it. Take it without too much breast-beating and weeping and wailing, "No fair!"* TAKE *it and* MAKE *it work for our own soul's growth.*

I can't believe you deliberately send it for that reason, God. But since we are stuck with it (or you are stuck with it) you will help see us through it. You will help us overcome it, and emerge purer, finer, better because of it. Above all, closer to you.

In personal suffering we can find you. Know you as never before.

As for other people's suffering? The appalling injustices we are forced to witness and before which we feel so impotent? These I cannot and must not ignore. These I must do all that I can to assuage.

Yet I cannot and must not let them stand between me and my God. To do so would only add my own misery to the weight of human despair. I must have you, God, to sustain me. I must have your help

*if I am to know any happiness as a human being, and so be able to
help anyone else.*

*My choice is this: "To doubt and do without," as someone has
said. Or "to believe and receive." I believe, Lord, I believe. And
even in times of trouble—yes, even more richly in times of trouble
—I receive!*

To Sing So That Others May Hear

One of the best articles I've ever read on suffering was written by
one of the two Hopes in my life, Hope Good; it appeared in the
magazine *Orion*. In it she told of once having a rabbit whose cage
was ripped apart by dogs one night and the pet torn to bits. She wept
for days, asking, "How could a loving God have permitted such a
catastrophe? Suddenly, like a revelation, I concluded that I was to
this creature as God is to me, yet I was unable to assist when it
needed me. Yes, God loves us with a deep compassion, even when
He is unable to come to our aid."

She went on to say, "We must stop asking, Why did this happen to
me? Instead, we must ask ourselves: How can I use it creatively?
. . . There is no evil so terrible that it cannot, with God's help, be
used . . . the challenge to make something of value replace a failure,
defeat or disappointment is about the only way man has to answer
the problem of suffering."

Another clipping, yellow with age. Written by former Senate chaplain Frederick Brown Harris in his column "Spires of the Spirit." He
called this one "Dialing the Man Upstairs." "The object in dialing
God is never to demand, 'Get me out of this,' but 'Save me from
surrendering to this.' We haven't mastered the first lesson in the
Primer of Life's meaning until we know that the chief end of man is
not comfort, but character. . . . If character were the goal, rather
than comfort, then a lot of things that otherwise seem to have no
business here would make some sense."

To become not bitter—but better. To compensate. To turn the af-
fliction into something fine. Artists always do this; a part of their
genius is the ability to translate their sufferings into their greatest
symphonies, sculpture, paintings, poems. But one needn't be a genius.
"Out of the night that covers me, / Black as the Pit from pole to
pole, / I thank whatever gods there may be / For my unconquerable

soul," my mother used to quote from "Invictus." And everyday, out of the dark night of suffering, shine forth unconquerable souls. With lights so vivid they brighten the way for others.

Two, of the many . . .

Barbie: Born with a clot which caused the blood to back up, to rupture and hemorrhage in the esophagus and stomach. Years of intense pain and stress, hospitalizations, surgeries—one to remove her esophagus and a third of her upper stomach. A last-ditch life-saving effort, which left a hole in her neck for saliva to drain out, and another hole made directly into her stomach through the abdomen into which liquids could be fed. Agonizing, weakening bouts with hiccuping . . . Yet this brave girl donned high-necked dresses, dated, went to school, held part-time jobs, sang in the choir—and wound up cheering those who came to cheer her!

During all this she was writing to her family and friends; remarkable letters which became a journal of courage and faith.

Listen to this, written at fifteen, after hearing a moving sermon about total commitment:

> I sat in the balcony in the "cry room" (for mothers with
> babies) where I could hear Pastor Bob but no one could
> hear me [hiccuping]. I sat up there half-drugged from
> my tranquilizers, angry, scared, and very discouraged. . . .
> Afterward, I went up to talk to him. He had told about
> a lady in his church who had tried to commit suicide
> before she'd found Christ and turned her life over to
> Him to control, and I wanted to know what he'd told HER.
> I told him I didn't understand why this had to happen
> to me again; and I asked him—if God is such a God of
> love, then why is He doing this to me? We talked
> for a while, then prayed together, and I went home to
> do just what he told me to.
>
> I went to my room and I prayed: "God, forgive my
> anger at You, and my discouragement. I know it's wrong,
> but I'm desperate, Lord. . . . Father, I give up fighting
> AGAINST having it—and fighting with You OVER it. If
> this is what You want for my life, even though I

don't understand it, I accept it. So here is my life for
You to do with whatever you want to. God, I believe
YOU'RE now in control. Thank You!"

Man, when you say that, look out—things are going to
start to happen!

She fell asleep without help for the first time in weeks, she relates,
and woke up hours later with the hiccups gone.

Now no one can tell me there is no God or that God is
dead or that He doesn't love and watch over His children.
I KNOW I have a God, and that my God is alive, and that my God
loves me!

Barbie's battle was far from over. At sixteen she was forced to
write, after unsuccessful surgery:

"Satan's cause is never more in danger than when a human
no longer desiring, but still intending to do God's will,
looks around him upon a universe from which every trace
of Him seems to have vanished, and asks why he has been
forsaken, and still obeys."

This quote from C. S. Lewis so perfectly depicts my
situation as I lay in the Intensive Care Unit. . . . I was
disappointed that the surgery had failed, terribly frustrated
that I was sick AGAIN, that I was born this way with no
hope of ever changing it, that I was missing out on
school activities, most of all I was just TIRED of hurting
so much!

Then the Lord stepped in and said, "Now wait a minute.
What is the last thing you did in that operating room before
you went to sleep?" I said, "Well, I committed my life
completely into your hands and thanked you in advance
for being my Sufficiency. . . . "O.K. then," He said. "What are
you getting so upset about? . . ."

She then prayed the famous Serenity Prayer: *God grant me the
serenity to accept the things I cannot change, the courage to change*

the things I can, and the wisdom to know the difference. And concluded:

> I can't change the fact that I was born with a birth
> defect, but I CAN change my attitude toward it.

Her high school picture smiles from the letter she wrote shortly before her eighteenth birthday. A radiantly beautiful dark-eyed girl, saying:

> It has now been 15 months since my esophagus had
> to be removed, and the doctors are still at a complete
> loss as to how to put me back together again. But
> in fulfilling His promise—"I can do all things through
> Christ who strengtheneth me"—it was made possible for
> me to combine my junior and senior years into one, and
> with the help of a wonderful tutor, to maintain a "B-plus"
> average, so I WILL walk down that aisle to receive my
> diploma with my class!

Barbie was almost nineteen when she wrote her final letter. Still intending to go to college, yet aware that the Lord might have other plans for her.

> Oh, Pastor Luther, I do praise and thank Him from
> my innermost being. Because as one of the verses
> from your text Sunday says, "They should SEEK the lord,
> if haply they might feel after Him and FIND Him, though
> He be NOT FAR FROM ANY ONE OF US. For in Him we live,
> and move, and have our being!" (See—I listened!!)
>
> . . . John 11:4 says, "This sickness is not unto death,
> but for the glory of God. . . ." But I'm not afraid to
> die, because if that is His ministry for me, then
> I am willing. And He CAN use me in this way, in
> EVERY way. . . . I am totally, completely His, to do
> with as He chooses.

The entire story of Barbie Hertel is being told in a book written by her mother. . . . Meanwhile, a school library building is being named for her, and the impact of her gallantry, her faith in the face of suffering, can never be measured.

Elias: A young Greek musician performing in a strange land. A slight limp, a long history of leg problems. Now—cancer, the doctors say. The limb must come off. . . . The night before the amputation he asks for his guitar. We bring it and he lies in bed tuning it lovingly. Then he begins to play and softly sing. Beautiful, heart-melting Grecian love songs. And it is so poignant and lovely the nurses begin to peer in. And other patients. They stand and listen, young and old. One a very old black man. And a young mother from her vigil in the children's wing.

Can she bring some children to hear him? she asks. Will he share his music with them? He says yes, of course, bring the children. And she comes leading them, three little girls who have had tracheotomies. Their throats are bandaged, none of them can speak. But they gaze at him with awed delight, these silent five- and six-year-olds. They keep time with their hands. And as the music quickens and he nods and smiles at them, one of them begins to dance around in her robe, her little slippers.

He leans toward them, his great dark eyes alight. "I play some songs you know, ha? You know 'Frère Jacques'?" They nod and he begins to sing, urging them to join in: "Frère *Jacq*ues . . . Frère *Jacq*ues—" And though they can't make a sound, their lips move, miming the words. With his smile and his eyes he encourages them.

Then he moves into one that makes them bounce: "This old man, he played *one,* he played nick-nack on my drum. . . . With a *nick-nack,* paddy-whack, give a dog a bone, *this* old man came rolling home!" They are beating time, the tiny one in pigtails tries to dance, too, mute but joyfully they "sing."

A sassy little black nurse pops in, joins the fun, warbling in a high foolish falsetto before ordering, "Now hold still, Mr. Music Man, for your shot." Attention is focused on the doomed leg lying in its heavy white cast. The foot protrudes, and into it the needle goes. Elias takes up his guitar again, finishes the next tune with the brisk familiar rhythm—"Shave and a haircut, six bits!" The children laugh and the one with the huge blue eyes clicks her tongue to echo its beat. Then, thanking him, the young mother shepherds them away.

Lights are being lowered, the others have left, too. We turn to tell him good night, each gripping a hand on either side of the bed. We say a little prayer for him. When his eyes open they are wet, but he continues to smile. "Now don't you worry, I be okay."

The next time we see him the leg is gone. He is in great pain. But he touches the tiny cross around his neck and forms the words silently, like the children—"I'm okay. I'm okay."

God Only Knows

Common expressions have a way of packaging truths.

Consider: "God only knows."

How often we say this when we come up against something we can't explain. Usually something we object to, something of which we despair. "Why did this have to happen? . . . God knows!" Or "God only knows."

Slang, yes . . . but wait, isn't it maybe something more? Can this be the voice of the soul itself speaking? Handing over to God a mystery too much for us. Saying, in essence—*God* knows . . . God *does* know. . . . And only God.

The speaker may not even be a believer, merely someone resigning the matter to fate. Yet the persistence of the soul's knowledge is there. . . . For we can't hope to understand all the secrets of the universe or the total nature of God or even of his complex creation, man.

We are so human. Faulty and finite. Boxed within certain physical limits, at least during our stay on earth. We can't fly in the air under our own power, or sustain ourselves under water unless we have aids. . . . And we have cleverly invented such aids; things we could not have imagined a few years ago we have now achieved. . . . Such progress! Yet how far are we able to progress in the matters of mind and spirit? How long will it take us to understand God?

Loving God and feeling his presence does not mean for a minute that we are his equals. . . . The maker of one single river . . . or the sun . . . or me! How can I hope to comprehend his mystery?

I just know that I am his child. And you are his child. And no matter what happens in this life or beyond it, he will not forsake us. . . . Meanwhile, when things occur that are beyond my feeble comprehension, things that test my faith, scald my spirit, rend my secret being, I can indeed cry out in sheer human dismay, resistant and yet resigned—yes, and reverent:

"God knows why. God only knows!"

While the still small voice of my deeper soul-knowledge whispers reassuringly: "Yes. God knows."

The Suffering Few of Us Escape

You know what a coward I am about suffering, God. My own or other people's.

I would never have made a martyr; once they started to beat me or drag me to the lions I'm afraid I'd have recanted. If I were imprisoned and they tortured me for secrets, I don't think I could stand it—I'd tell!

And I am sickened before the spectacle of suffering, any physical suffering, of man or animal. (How can anyone be entertained by brutal acts? How can anyone cheer at the sight of any creature bruised, bleeding, struggling desperately to escape?)

It's hard for me even to READ *about suffering. If I am helpless to stop it, it seems witless to punish my own flesh and soul by drinking in the dread details. . . .*

No, no, I must flee from physical suffering.

Yet there is another kind of suffering few of us can flee. And that we cannot stop by a mere act of will: not by averting our eyes, running away, slamming the door.

The agony of love in all its variations.

Man and woman love. The many aspects of love between male and female . . . Anxiety about the one so close to us . . . Long separations . . . Conflicts, quarrels, doubts . . . Husband and wife who've forgotten how to talk to each other . . . Indifference . . . The bitter wounds of unfaithfulness . . . To be denied the person most deeply loved . . . The awful unfulfilled hungers of body and soul . . .

These our private crucifixions.

And children: O God, dear God, the multiple crucifixions we undergo for our children. Nailed to the cross again and again for their shortcomings. Or only waiting at the cross sometimes (which can be worse) forced to witness their suffering.

So I am no stranger to suffering. And I can't honestly call myself a coward before these emotional assaults. In some ways I feel brave before them. I have faced them before, most of them, and will face them again and survive. You give me the strength, you give me the courage.

You make me realize that anyone who drinks from the sweet cup of love must also swallow the gall. But love is worth it . . . ah, but it's worth it! And if you are truly love, as Jesus taught, then the price we pay for love has even more value.

In suffering for love of others we are also suffering for love of you. This suffering I welcome, Lord.

If It Can Teach Us to Forgive

My heart broke for this daughter, so young to be suffering so much. The *if onlys* piled up . . . *If only* we could have talked them out of the too-early marriage. *If only* we'd had the right answers or been able to help when the problems got bad . . .

But now the worst of it is over, and she emerges from the years of trial still young and calm and strong and—incredibly—even closer to God: "Mother, listen, just because we love God and he loves us doesn't mean we're not going to have *pain*. Pain is the price we pay on earth for loving someone. But the pain of love—that's the kind of pain that can make us realize the true nature of God.

"How could I turn my back on Jesus just because I have suffered over human love? I understand now how *he,* Jesus, feels. How he must suffer over loving us so much, when so many people don't know or love him."

She speaks of her marriage without regret; they both learned so much from each other. "And who knows what time will bring? Who knows the impact we have on other lives? Who knows what God can do, how much good he can build out of our mistakes? The fact that we could forgive each other for the pain we caused each other, isn't that what Jesus wants? Isn't that a pretty big thing? Yes, of course it hurts, but even hurting isn't in vain if it can teach us to forgive."

God Says, "Get Up!"

Again and again God says, "Get up!"

Sometimes he speaks through people, and it seems a harsh, unfeeling physical command. . . . I am ill. Pain-wracked. Anyone can see I'm in no condition to leave my bed. Yet the doctor and the nurses enter, and to my astonishment say, "Let's get you up awhile today. You must get up."

Sometimes it is but the voice of the stern but loving command of the God without and within. . . . I am prostrate with grief, my life is in shambles, there is nothing left for me now but the terrible comfort of my tears. . . . Dimly, beyond drawn shades, I realize the world is going on heartlessly about its business. People pass by, some of them even laughing, outside on the street. . . . The telephone rings. There is a knocking at my door.

I stuff my ears, try to burrow deeper into my awful loss. Then the voice comes strong and clear: "Get up."

"I can't, I can't. . . . O God, I can't."

It comes again. This time more imperative than the telephone or the doorbell or the awareness of duties to people who need me. *"Get up!"*

Startled, I stagger to my feet. . . . Grope protestingly for some means of support—and find it. A chair to lean on, or unexpectedly the arm of a friend . . . But in a few minutes I realize I won't need them, for there is another support beside me. God has provided the brace. He would not call me back to action otherwise. He will sustain me.

It is so easy to "quench my thirst with tears and so learn to love my sorrows," as the Paulist priest James Carroll wrote. So easy, and often so tempting, to fall in love with our own misfortunes. For that way lies sympathy (if sometimes only self-sympathy) and possible escape. . . .

We're tired, fed up with this rat race, this drudgery; we don't want to work. . . . "Get up. Do it!"

We are ill and nurturing our own illness. . . . "Get up. Get well."

We are stricken with sorrow or shame; our troubles overpower us, we long only to sink into the slough of our despondency behind

locked doors. . . . The command rings loud and clear: "You cannot bury yourself any longer. Get up! Get on with living."

Again and again Jesus said those words. To people lying in sick-
beds or even on deathbeds: "Arise! Get up." And they did, and
were well and lived again. He is saying them still to anyone who
will listen: "Don't give in to your pain and problems. Don't nourish
your grief. Get up."

Thank you, Lord, for never failing to say them to me.

*Life is too short and too sweet to squander in the darkness,
crying. Thank God, thank God you always get me up and back into
action. This, as nothing else could, proves how much you care for
me.*

The Crosses

Morning . . . a broad green Iowa pasture where the children and
I used to hike . . . Crawl gingerly under the barbed-wire fence,
then up the hill and on through the tall tossing grasses. Lurking
among this growth are the lavender thistles, pronged and pert, like
imps to be wary of. Birds spurt ahead—quails and blackbirds red-
winged and gold. Meadow larks call from the fences. Everywhere
the bird cries are ringing and chirring and caroling. How many there
are—a bird Paradise.

The green-golding weeds and grasses have a gilded look in the
morning sun. They wash and shine and make their own soft music.
They bend toward the bank. The ground pitches toward this bank,
and at its edge you look down upon the stream, broad and clear and
sparkling, winding between these escarpments. In the distance more
fields, and the houses of the town Le Mars, and highways where
cars and a few trucks race along. Yet here all is wide and vast,
peaceful and free.

I walk along the bank and then down its side to be near the water,
where there are glittering sandy beaches, and then thick muddy
tracks where the cows have been. The mud is very black and rutted
from their hooves; it squishes underfoot and sinks softly, and my
sneakers turn black at the edge. I plod along until I reach the
dry place and then consider climbing back. . . . And standing there

wondering which is the least steep, I am aware of telephone poles that swing along the division between pasture and plowed cornfield. Poles standing slender and tall and spread-armed against the sky.

Or are they telephone poles? Utility poles probably, because they have a crosspiece, they make the form of the cross. And at the tip of each arm and at its crest is a small ornament that must have something to do with power. A glass insulator, maybe? Whatever it is, it adorns this cross—these gentle, graceful, stately crosses as they repeat themselves, at first large . . . then smaller . . . smaller . . . dwindling to the eye against the sky.

For some reason I start up the steepest bank, and discover it isn't very steep, after all. Following a slightly zigzag course, I go bounding to the top. . . . And stand arrested once more by the sight of the crosses through which the silent power sings.

The image of the cross itself is enhanced. . . . Is man driven, I wonder, to repeat this design in so many areas of his life? Or is it that the cross was and remains a plain, practical arrangement of timbers or anything else, to support death . . . or life? In any case, here are these simple, lovely crosses against the blue morning country sky. And I am held by the sight.

The cross, symbol of sin and suffering—this beautiful geometrical design. And comfort and inspiration to so many . . . Christ suffered for us and he took away our sins. But he couldn't spare us the suffering; not even he! Yet isn't the empty cross the symbol of suffering that is over and done with? Of the man who died there and then walked free?

I understand now what my friend Hope Applebaum meant when she said once, "You have to suffer. You have to go through Gethsemane before you can rise." At the time I knew what she was saying but it had no real significance. Now it seems as clear and clean as the country air. . . . All these crosses! They mark the landscape of our lives.

Even as I stand there looking at the utility poles I see that they have double arms. There are crosses piled upon crosses. . . . We often carry several crosses at a time. And yet each is gemmed with its little vital star of power. And the time eventually comes when that particular cross has served its purpose; the hour of suffering is over and the cross is empty. The man or woman walks free.

Now that I have become aware of crosses I see them wherever I am. Fashioning a child's kite, looking up at the mast of a sailing ship—always the central spire and the arms outspread. It is an image of balance and beauty, of both surrender and blessing.

And the crosses in all the windows of the world! The shape of the cross that is made by the central lines of windowpanes . . . Coming into an English village one night at sunset, the winding streets so narrow you could almost reach out from the bus and touch the cottages on either side . . . and each cottage window ablaze with the sun, as if to illuminate the black crosses that divide the glass.

It was like suddenly seeing a whole forest of small black crosses alight to welcome us. I said to my daughter, "Look, look!" And she, too, saw the phenomenon. Not only here but every place we went—on the streets of London, in the windows of loft or shop or pub, the cross as clearly defined, once you watch for it, as on the spires of cathedrals.

All those crosses, like a silent signal, inescapable, reassuring. Reminding us of the many trials people can endure and yet every day go cheerfully on . . .

But let's not get too poetic about crosses. They are beautiful from a distance, yes. During those times of life when we have put ours down (if only for a little rest); when we've grown enough to know the value, get perspective . . . But when you're *carrying* one! (Or more.)

The thing to remember is this: We are not alone. Each of us has a cross to bear. The fact that we may not see another person's cross, often don't even suspect it, doesn't mean it isn't there. Hidden, so often bravely hidden behind a smile, a laugh, a proud carriage, a job superbly done—hidden behind locked doors—yet the cross is there. Again and again I have been staggered at the eventual revelations. Shocked to discover how many people had been going through their private crucifixions . . .

Crucifixions for others. Parents crucified for their children's mistakes. The husband or wife of an alcoholic crucified hour by hour. Not intentionally—few people deliberately set out to hurt those close to them—yet the inevitable Golgotha is there. So many, oh so many innocent victims! Nailed to the cross of our terrible concern for those we love, we bleed for them, and there is no freedom for our tormented spirits until they, too, are free.

Yet doesn't this, too, draw us closer to God? By sharing Christ's cup of suffering don't we taste the true communion? And if we can love as he loved, forgive as he forgave, we, too, can be uplifted.

No personal crucifixion need ever be in vain.

Cut Back the Vines

"Go cut back the grapes," I tell my son. "They're too thick, they've practically taken over the garage."

Naturally he has urgent business elsewhere; but after the usual argument he grabs the pruning shears and dashes outdoors. I hear him whacking away.

I look out later, and am aghast. The garage walls are naked. He has severed the lush growth clear back to the ground. "You've ruined them!" I accuse. "We'll never have grapes there again."

Wrong. The grapes came back the following year with an abundance never known before; great purple clusters, fat and sweet, so heavy they bowed the trellis. It was just as Jesus said: "Every branch in me that beareth not fruit he taketh away: and every branch that beareth fruit, he purgeth it, that it may bring forth more fruit" (John 15:2).

I thought of the ruthless slashing. The seeming waste. My scolding protests and my son's innocent bewilderment—he'd thought it was what I wanted. Our misunderstanding. The great fire we had to have even to dispose of the old branches . . . And now this! The newer, stronger, invigorated vines. The harvest so plentiful we carried basketsful to the neighbors.

"He purgeth it. . . ." Pain and problems, the conflicts and disappointments, the defeats, the tragedies to which we all are subject—are they not purgings? I look back on my life sometimes in amazement before the memories of those terrible cuttings. Those times of trial by fire, it seemed . . . Intolerable, intolerable. Rescue me, spare me! . . . Yet now I realize they were essential to my growth. How much hostility had to go in the process, how much self-pity, how much pride. A tangle of choking, life-impeding habits threatening to deny all that God meant me to be. I, too, had to be cut back, laid low.

And somehow, in the midst of it, I realized I could not go it alone, Lord. It was too much. I could not handle the weight of it, the people, the problems, the family, my job as a wife and mother, my fate as a woman in this demanding world, without support beyond my own.

Those words in John—all of them—must have been written for me: "Abide in me, and I in you. As the branch cannot bear fruit of itself, except it abide in the vine; no more can ye, except ye abide in me.

"I am the vine, ye are the branches: He that abideth in me, and I in him, the same bringeth forth much fruit: for without me ye can do nothing" (John 15:4–5).

It was like that. I saw that without you I could do nothing. You are the vine, not me. Weak and faulty as I was, I'd been trying to be the vine, holding up all the branches. I was just a branch and I had to be pruned, I had to be stripped if my roots were to be strengthened. Then only then could I bring forth much fruit!

Persecution

It is a common paradox that persecution only intensifies faith. Strange. Why? Does God release some extra dimension of power when things get really rough?

Those early Christians, stoned, whipped, burned . . . What sustained them? What gave them the courage to suffer and die? But more, seeing their fate, what kept the rest of them from turning traitor? Instead, the very blood shed seemed to nourish the Christian soil, new converts sprang up.

What would have happened to Christianity without opposition? I wonder. Supposing the Romans and Greeks and unconverted Jews had said, "Okay, go ahead, don't mind us." Supposing they'd built churches instead of hiding out to worship in caves and homes? Would they have preached with such passion? Could they have drawn others to the cross if they hadn't been forced to carry their own—and to die on them? Supposing it had all been made easy. Would Christianity have become the living force it has been through the ages? Would it even have survived?

In our own time—the persecutions in communist countries . . .

the Soviet Union, East Germany, Albania, Czechoslovakia, Yugoslavia . . . people crowd into darkened homes. To share a single Bible, to pray and sing. Sometimes just to listen to someone who *remembers* the Bible. And when he comes, this Dutchman who can be known only as Brother Andrew, with the Bibles he has been able to smuggle across the border, carefully rationing them out—they weep for joy and risk arrest to have one in their possession. . . .

(My church is never locked. There are half a dozen churches within walking distance of my house. I have more versions of the Bible than I can count. What do they matter? Really *matter?* I can go to church or read a Bible anytime I want—so I put it off. . . . No, it isn't ease that intensifies faith, it is desperation and denial.)

God's Smuggler. Richard Wurmbrand's *Underground Saints*. And that other staggering book of Wurmbrand's, *In God's Underground* . . . These modern martyrs—I read their stories of sacrifice, imprisonment, torture, the incredible things they are still undergoing for God, and am ashamed. My own problems pale. I have never been persecuted. I have never suffered, at least not like that.

Could I if I had to, Lord?

This is not to say that you or I or God would willingly inflict such torment on anyone. But we must recognize that good can come of it. That there is no evil so terrible that good can't come of it. And sometimes a stark, bone-deep realization of how much God really means to us can come in no other way.

We turn to God, too, as individuals or en masse when all hope seems lost and there *is* no other way. (Why not *from* God when even he seems unable to deliver us from the tangible evil? Why *to?*)

Stalin's "planned and deliberate famine" intended to break the peasants' resistance to collectivization. . . . Malcolm Muggeridge describes the terrible toll in *Chronicles of Wasted Time*. And how he went to a crowded church one morning in Kiev, after witnessing it.

> Young and old, peasants and townsmen, parents
> and children . . . Never before or since have I
> participated in such worship; the sense
> conveyed of turning to God in great affliction

was overpowering . . . for instance where the
congregation say there is no help for them
save from God. What intense feeling they
put into those words! In their minds, I
knew, as in mine, was a picture of those
desolate abandoned villages, of the hunger
and the hopelessness, of the cattle trucks
being loaded with humans in the dawn light.

Where were they to turn for help? Not to
the Kremlin and the Dictatorship of the
Proletariat, certainly; nor to the forces
of progress and democracy and enlightenment
in the West. . . . Every possible human agency
found wanting. So only God remained, and to
God they turned with a passion, a dedication,
a humility, impossible to convey. They took
me with them; I felt closer to God then than
I ever had before, or am likely to again.

Such reactions are intuitive, leading to truths too profound to
question. They go back beyond time, back to Job and Lamentations
and the hillsides where David sang his songs of worshipful desperation: "I cried unto the Lord with my voice, and he heard me out of
his holy hill. Selah. I laid me down and slept; I awakened; for the
Lord sustained me. I will not be afraid of ten thousands of people,
that have set themselves against me . . ." (Psalm 3:4–6).

It is as if we are led by strong supernal forces. Driven by the
soul's surest wisdom: This way, this way! "Come unto me, all ye
that labour and are heavy laden, and I will give you rest" (Matt.
11:28).

God's Answer to Evil

Isn't the strength that is born of suffering God's answer to evil?
God does not will the suffering, cannot or does not prevent it, cannot
or does not always take it from us. But within each of us he has implanted a precious core of power mightier than the atom. Call it
what you will, survival mechanism maybe, the stubborn will to

overcome. But trigger it, arouse it, stir it with enough pain and despair and humiliation, enflame it, feed it with human blood, and look out. The explosion can rock the world.

It happened in a mass sense with our black people; and it happens in an individual sense every day. Jaws jutted, teeth bared, eyes flashing, human beings emerge from hell to declare: "Nothing is impossible to me now!"

Somewhere at this moment—on a hospital bed or in a prison cell . . . at a machine or desk, in a mill or mine where even a job can seem punishment . . . in a divorce court or the purgatory of a loveless marriage . . . in the cruel tearings of family conflict—there are new people being born. Coming forth stronger and finer. Seeing themselves, perhaps for the first time, in all their reality and true potential.

"The best years of your life may be the years of your failure, your heartbreak, your loneliness," wrote Air Force Chaplain Thomas E. Myers before his own death in a crash with his men. "When you discover *why* you have life and go one step further, decide that no matter what cost may be involved, you will follow that *why* until you see yourself the 'man God meant.' . . . You will have found that special thing which the God who made you planned for only you to build, to create, to cause to grow."

That may be one "reason" for suffering. Never God-caused but forever God-used, if we but have the courage to turn to that source implanted within us.

For Every Cross I've Carried

Thank you, God, for every cross I have ever had to carry. For every burden I have ever had to bear. For every honest tear I have ever shed.

Thank you for my troubles—they give me courage.

Thank you for my afflictions—they teach me compassion.

Thank you for my disappointments—through them I learn humility and am inspired to try harder again.

Thank you that in fashioning this world you didn't see fit to spare us from the evil you knew would be there. Thank you for not keeping us like dumb animals in a corral. That, instead, you freed us, gave us the dignity of making our own decisions, even if it also meant we must stumble and fall and suffer in order to rise again.

Thank you that in every aspect of our lives you are always near us. Loving, protecting, helping. Hearing our prayers and giving us the strength to endure what we must for our own souls' growth.

I know you, Lord, in times of peace and plenty. But when life is easy it's too easy to forget you; I don't need you quite so much. When life is tough, however, when I see nothing about me but trouble and torment, then I must find you, I must have you! I go crying to you through the darkness, knowing that though the whole world forsake me you will not turn away.

My very suffering brings you near.

The Holy Spirit

And ye shall receive the gift of the Holy Ghost.
For the promise is unto you, and to your children.

Acts 2:38–39

The Holy Spirit

William V. Rauscher says: "We are souls with bodies, not merely bodies with souls." Prayer is the voice of the soul speaking to its source. And the soul, to our own amazement, may speak a different language.

I must talk about the Holy Spirit.

I realize this subject is controversial. It may send some people running, with their hands over their ears. I beg that they listen, only listen, as I had to learn to listen. What I have to say and to share may help make more real the presence of God:

Childhood memories of church . . . and the story of Pentecost. Again and again I heard it told, always with great reverence and conviction: How, after the ascension—just as Jesus had promised—on the day of Pentecost, when a large group of his followers were gathered in one place—

> And suddenly there came a sound from heaven as of a
> rushing mighty wind, and it filled all the house where
> they were sitting.
>
> And there appeared unto them cloven tongues like
> as of fire, and it sat upon each of them.
>
> And they were all filled with the Holy Ghost, and
> began to speak with other tongues, as the Spirit gave
> them utterance. (Acts 2:2–4)

And how a multitude of other people, people of different nationalities,

> were confounded, because that every man heard them
> speak in his own language. . . .
>
> And they were all amazed,
> and were in doubt, saying one to another, What meaneth
> this? (Acts 2:6, 12)

"Others mocking said, These men are full of new wine." And how Peter stood up to assure them,

"These are not drunken, as ye suppose. . . ."

I can still hear my mother's voice, bless her—a wonderful Sunday school teacher—echoing that indignant protest: "These men are not drunken!" Then, gently, "They simply could not *understand* that it was a fulfillment of what Jesus had foretold—they could do wonderful things because they were filled with the Holy Ghost."

And we would all file out of church thinking what a shame it was (if we thought about it any further) that outsiders could so misjudge such a remarkable thing.

Still—the Holy Ghost . . . Three services on Sunday, countless prayer meetings and revivals in between—yet in all my years in this fundamentalist church (which I still love) I never had the faintest clue as to what Holy Ghost was supposed to be or do for us. Something to do with the Trinity (whatever *that* was). God and Jesus—those I could comprehend. But *Holy* sounded scary and *Ghost* sounded worse. Even the preachers weren't specific; in fact they seemed to back away from it. . . . Maybe because of people like the Pentecostals.

Only a handful in our town, but hundreds came every summer for meetings in the old Chautauqua pavilion. Holy Rollers, we called them, because of their antics—shouting and sometimes running down the aisles and flinging themselves into the sawdust at the front. It was great fun to go and watch them. Did they speak in unknown tongues? I don't remember. But they did a lot of yelling and one woman would hold up her hand for hours, as if paralyzed.

Disgraceful. Nutty . . . No, we didn't doubt Pentecost for a minute. But Pentecostals were crazy.

These men are drunken . . . these men are full of new wine.

We heard no accusing echoes.

John

Not until years later did this mysterious "being" (?), "person" (?), "power" (?), even come to my attention. Through John. The derelict (though I wince to call him that—he proved to be a saint) who appeared at the door of the enormous Victorian house we had just bought and were attempting to remodel after a move to Washington,

D.C. . . . A preposterous job which the children and I were struggling with alone.

And there he was one day, announcing: "Ma'am, looks like you
need an extra pair of hands." He was broke, he said, a painter by
trade, and would work for a dollar an hour.

At noon, spreading papers to picnic on the bare floor, we asked
him to join us. "Thanks kindly, ma'am." He sat down and bowed
his head. Then, lifting his eyes and accepting a sandwich, he said:
"You know the Lord sent me to you." (Oh boy, a religious nut—
that's all we need!) "When I woke up at the mission this morning
I prayed I would be led to somebody I could really help. And I
spent my last dime for the bus and rode till the Lord told me to get
off. And I walked a block and here you were!"

Drinking had been his downfall we learned in the weeks that
followed—weeks blessed in more ways than one. The dark wood-
work bloomed behind his brush, he transformed the walls with
bright paper, sanded and restored the ancient floors. . . . And we
talked. . . . He had been saved almost a year ago at a Pentecostal camp meeting down South. "Went in drunk, came out sober,
and have been sober ever since. I felt the Lord's hand on my shoulder—believe it or not, ma'am, I *felt* it. And a mighty fire went
through me and I like to fainted, but I could hear the Lord's voice
just as plain as I hear you, in my ear. And he told me: 'You're
ready now, John.'"

Each time we paid him my husband and I wondered if he would
make it through the weekend. We hoped so, terribly, not only for
our sake but for his. He had told us that when his year was up he
was heading back down South. "If I can honestly tell them I've been
sober for a year they'll write my name down in a book."

He was a chain smoker, to his intense regret. "But the Lord says,
'One thing at a time, John. I'll let you know when you're strong
enough to quit.'"

He helped us and we helped him. And he began to help others at
the mission. "This fella he was beat and sick, but I took him to my
room and prayed with him. We got down on our knees by my bed
and prayed that he'd be better in the morning and what's more find
a job and a decent place to live. And this morning he was! And I
give him one of those suits of your husband's—I hope you don't
mind—and we found this ad in the newspaper, this restaurant that

needed a dishwasher, and I took him there and they hired him. They even give him a room right there! I tell you, ma'am, when you got the Lord inside you and really trust him he don't let you down."

Something tore at my heart . . . some awful compassion. The blind leading the blind . . . the lost leading the lost.

His bland blue eyes, meek, respectful, yet filled with some great dignity, regarded me. "If you'll pardon my saying so, ma'am, to us the Comforter is real. It's like—well, the less you have, the less trouble God's got getting through. Folks like you—you have so much. Your family, your home, your car, everything—especially your self-respect. You just don't *need* the Holy Ghost so much."

The Holy Ghost? I winced.

John was looking so nice and doing so well we decided, in our ignorance, to do something more for John. Our church, a lovely Episcopal church, was right next door. We asked John if he wouldn't like to attend there with us. Though I shouldn't have been, I was surprised when he shook his head: "No thanks, ma'am, I wouldn't feel at home. If you'll excuse me being so frank, regular churches are just too formal and polite. When a man's poor and down and out, when he's got a crying need for God he's got to feel free to cry right out in meeting when he feels the Spirit on him."

The house was finally finished; John took another job. It was months before we saw him again. Then one cold morning the doorbell rang. "John!" I almost embraced him. "Come in."

He came, shy and deferential as always, but with that flat quality of assurance he had—and something else, something newly proud. I was just having coffee. I poured him a cup, surprised he didn't immediately light up. "Can I find you a cigarette?" I asked.

"No thanks, ma'am. The other night in meeting the Lord told me it was time to quit. Just like he said he would. He spoke in my ear: 'Okay, John, you're ready now.'" The mild blue eyes regarded me over his cup. "Three weeks ago that was. I threw away a whole pack that night and ain't touched a one since."

He had come to tell me good-by, he said. Cold weather and all, he was heading back for Natchez. "Besides, now my year is up. Better than a year—a year and two months, to be exact. But I figure I better play safe. I want to be *sure,*" he grinned, "when they write my name in that book. But now I don't have to worry, now that I can give up them cigarettes."

He rose and held out his hand. "Thank you for everything, ma'am."

"We're the ones to be grateful, John!"

He started down the porch steps on his long, oddly graceful stride; then suddenly he turned, hesitated, blurted—"I hope you don't mind if I pray for you, ma'am?"

"Why, no, that's wonderful. And I'll pray for you, too."

He stood biting his lips. His eyes were wet. "I'm going to pray that the Lord will git you safely home."

Hope

Hope . . . At first a neighbor, then a friend. Then as close as my own sister. One of those women every woman has to have to keep her sanity sometimes—someone to whom you can safely pour out your heart. But more—intelligent, dear, and deep. We could discuss books as ardently as personal problems; she knew and cared about things that matter, art and philosophy and music and religion. Yet I had known her more than a year before she revealed one of the most significant aspects of her life.

I had been telling her about John. His strange words at parting. "There he was in that clean but shabby overcoat we'd given him, not as warm as it should be for that cold day, setting out to *hitch-hike* clear to Mississippi. Because it meant so much to him to have a preacher write his name in a *book!*" As I had choked up that day, shutting the door in my bewilderment, my eyes brimmed now, remembering. "And here I was in the big warm home he'd made so beautiful for us, dutifully going to that big beautiful church next door—and he could say *that!*"

"He was filled with the Spirit, Marj. The Holy Spirit. He had had the Baptism and he wants you to share the joy of being at home with the Comforter."

I gazed at her dumbly (after all those years in church) and she began to explain. How a Pentecostal experience can miraculously change lives. How a neo-Pentecostal force, known as the charismatic movement, was sweeping the country, bringing nonbelievers to Jesus, and waking up gone-to-sleep Christians into a new awareness of his reality through the Baptism in the Spirit.

"It's a very real experience physically and emotionally. And it's accompanied by some of the gifts of the Spirit described in the New Testament, usually the gift of tongues." She paused. "This happened to me, Marj. Quite a while ago, before we met."

"But you're not Pentecostal, you're Presbyterian!"

"I'm a Christian. Pentecost belongs to all of us. You don't have to jump around about it, go to extremes, but the Holy Spirit was sent for all of us. He didn't pack up his bags and go back to heaven when the Bible was finished, although that's where most churches have tried to keep him. Jesus said over and over we all must be born again, of the water *and the Spirit*. And the Bible says, 'The promise is unto you, and to your children, and to all that are afar off.' That means us, too, now, today!"

She told me of the first time she had spoken in tongues, quite alone at home, and unexpectedly. "I had been studying and thinking about it but I hadn't thought it could happen to *me*." She laughed. "I thought I might be getting unbalanced, so I called my sister, who's an ordained Presbyterian minister. She said it was valid, it was happening in her own congregation, but to be careful, not going around telling people. Most people wouldn't understand, they might think you *were* crazy."

I went home shaken, filled with a new respect and love for my friend that bordered on awe. To be so quiet and unassuming about something so marvelous. It seemed to me she must be rare and special to be chosen for such a gift from God. Reading the books and articles she gave me didn't change my opinion. (Among them John Sherrill's classic *They Speak with Other Tongues* and the wonderful booklet *The Holy Spirit,* by J. A. Dennis.)

I was fascinated by the whole phenomenon—and so were a lot of other people, I discovered. Yet it remained a marvel I could only admire and share vicariously.

We had moved to the suburbs now, saw less of each other, yet talked often by phone. And it was on the telephone that Hope first prayed for me in tongues. Some of the most beautiful sounds I've ever heard—like music, swift and sweet and clear, oriental in tone. When it stopped she said simply, "Praise the Lord! You are going to get some rest and feel better now."

And I did.

Once when we hadn't seen each other for several months we met in the city for lunch. We were scarcely seated when she put down her napkin and exclaimed, "Oh, I feel the Spirit upon me!" Her face was radiant as she leaned across the table and began to prophesy: about changes that were coming into my work; about a book I hadn't even told her I had begun. Prophecies that seemed incredible at the time, but that were to come amazingly true.

This is not to be confused with divination or fortunetelling. The Old Testament is filled with its God-inspired prophets—they even foretold what would happen in the New. While on the day of Pentecost Peter stated, speaking for God: "I will pour out of my Spirit upon all flesh: and your sons and your daughters shall prophesy. . . ."

So I believed in the Baptism and did not doubt its gifts, not only of tongues but of healing and interpretation and prophecy. Hadn't they come to my dearest friend? And although a part of me envied her, I was content to bask in the glow.

Melanie

Melanie . . . our last late child. So blond, so lithe and lovely, jumping her horse, tripping off to ballet school. Fun to talk to—about dates and life and self, with perceptions so far beyond her years they sometimes sent me flying for my notebook . . . But no longer interested in church; refusing even to participate in the young people's activities . . . Plead, insist, fight about it, make her go? I was too tired—or cowardly. Afraid of alienating her further, as I once felt I had been alienated by all the religion stuffed down me.

Then during her senior year she was hospitalized as doctors sought the cause for a chronic low-grade fever and fatigue. (Mononucleosis? They never did find out.) She'd read everything else around, so one day I took her John Sherrill's book and some others on tongues. When I went back she was sitting up, excited. "And you say Hope can do *that?* Oh, Mommy, it must be wonderful!"

Commencement . . . Visiting colleges . . . Choosing one in Boston where she could concentrate on her beloved dancing . . . Fall and time to buy clothes. She'd always admired Hope from a little distance—Mother's friend; the admiration enhanced now by this sense of mystery. . . . A few days before she was to leave for Boston, doing final shopping downtown, Melanie said suddenly:

"Mother, I'd love to talk to Hope before I go. Let's ask her to have lunch with us."

I called Hope's office. She couldn't or be with us for dinner either. But if we could meet her at five o'clock? The most quiet and convenient place was the cocktail lounge of a nearby hotel. We chose a corner, ordered coffee. And there, of all places, my daughter and my friend had one of the most beautiful conversations of any of our lives. I don't remember a word of what was said, only that I sat rejoicing. For I knew that something significant was happening. And at its close Hope took my daughter's hand and prayed for her softly in tongues.

We all sort of floated onto the street. Melanie's face was shining. She turned to Hope to say good-by. "I want this, too," she said. "Where can I go to find it?"

Hope told her the name of a small nondenominational charismatic church she sometimes attended. They met for prayer every Wednesday night. This was Tuesday. "Mother, may I go?"

"Of course, if you think you have the time."

"I'll take the time. And, if you don't mind, I want to go by myself."

The next day I heard her canceling a final date. She dressed as carefully, however, as if she were going out with a new boy. But she seemed so *young,* climbing into the car to set out on so vital a journey all alone. . . . I flew down after her. "Honey, are you sure you don't want me to go along?"

She nodded emphatically. Looking a little scared but determined, she was off down the drive.

Toward ten o'clock the telephone rang. "Mother?" The voice was filled with elation. "I've received the Baptism!"

The experience changed her life. I am convinced that on one occasion it actually saved her life.

Months later I shared the story with a distinguished woman writer, one whose books are found in every church library, almost every home. I wasn't sure she would approve. To my relief her response was quick and fervent: "I can't think of a more valuable thing to happen to a girl about to go away to college." She went on to tell me not only she herself but a number of prominent religious leaders had had the Baptism and were encouraging others to seek it, make it a living force in their lives. "As for speaking in tongues, it *isn't* just gobbledy-gook as some people think, and not always just an unknown heavenly language. Very often others, and not just interpreters either, recognize it as their native tongue just as people did on that first day at Pentecost."

She told of an incident when a missionary couple were to speak to a large crowd of mainly unlettered people in the Philippines. "We would call them peasants. And the Holy Spirit came upon a lot of them and they began to speak in tongues. My friends themselves were astounded. They went down among them and found many of them speaking French and Spanish and perfect Oxford English."

Such demonstrations are borne out by a letter received by Bob Topping, pastor of the Church of Northern Virginia, where Melanie received her Baptism. It was written by Father Matthew from Holy Cross Abbey, Berryville, Virginia:

> Dear Bob: I wish to express my gratitude to you for coming here and giving us the Baptism of the Holy Spirit. Yesterday Brother Emmanuel spoke in tongues at our prayer meeting and it gave us great confidence. Then yesterday afternoon I did so for the first time. May God be praised! I know two of the others are on the threshold. We are filled with joy here and the new depths of charity are almost tangible. It is with great awe and expectation we await the revelation of God's mission for us as a group. . . . It was during your prayer I heard the gift of tongues for the first time. I recognized the language you spoke. I had heard it often at the Russicum in Rome and at the Monastery of Chevetogne in Belgium. It was the old Slavonic used in the Russian Orthodox liturgy. Was it not significant that you, a Protestant, and I and the other Catholics, were praying before the Russian icons and the Holy Spirit should use Russian tongue to express His prayer? May it be the first fruits of the coming unity, the Spirit of all Christians and also the prelude to the brotherhood between the American and Russian people. . . .

Back to Melanie . . . .

It was quite late when she walked in that night, still in a high state of elation. She'd taken a wrong turn and gotten lost. "But they warned me something like this could happen. The devil doesn't want to lose you, he'll do everything he can to upset you and make you doubt. But you'll be protected. And oh, Mother, it's so *wonderful!* To love God this much, and know Jesus is inside you giving you this beautiful gift, your own way to reach him and praise him."

This—from the same girl who'd pulled a pillow over her head when I begged her to get up and go to church? It was almost too much. And now it was she who became the persuader:

"And it's so available. To everybody! So easy. Just *ask* for it and let yourself go and it will happen. Don't keep holding back."

So easy? For the young—yes, those who can go zooming into new challenges without a backward glance. But once you're older and habit-hammered, wrapped firmly in life's familiar packaging with the cords pulled tight . . . I believed in it implicitly, frequently attended services where it was practiced (always in perfect order as the Bible commands), proclaimed my discovery to others. Always adding hastily, "Of course it hasn't happened to *me,* and I doubt if it will—but I know it's invaluable to everyone who has it." Not admitting even to myself how much I longed for this indubitable proof of God's existence . . . Not that I really doubted any more—I was far beyond that. Just that I hungered for some vivid, tangible evidence of his reality in my life.

Yet when others went into the prayer room for the laying on of hands, I was too shy. Too self-conscious. Something in me resisted the thought of anything so personal—to me, at least, so private—as surrender to God, being witnessed even by the finest people. I couldn't, that's all. And I didn't know how to do it by myself.

At first Melanie, by phone or letter, urged me to get rid of these inhibitions. "Don't you realize God's offering you something very precious and you're turning your back?" Then after a while she gave up and began to see it Hope's way. . . . Hope, who could understand me as a woman:

"There are many ways to worship, Marj, and other gifts of the Spirit. Surely some not even mentioned in the Bible. You already have one of them, your writing. You are reaching people by speaking clearly, why worry about speaking in tongues?"

True, yes, and consoling. Settle for what you have, and be grateful. Yet the longing remained. . . . Then Melanie had an experience that jolted me into a new awareness of the power of the Holy Spirit.

One night, coming down the steps from the apartment she shared with some girls, a man emerged from the shadows, grabbed her, and attempted to drag her into the alley. In the violent ensuing struggle she called out aloud for God's help, and began to speak in tongues.

Instantly her assailant released her. And backed away . . .

However, as she ran sobbing down the street, the man pursued her, caught her, and began to struggle with her again. And again she cried out to God and spoke in tongues.

This time, muttering amazement, the man let her go completely, turned, and fled. By the time she reached safety he had vanished.

She is convinced—and I will always be—the Holy Spirit overpowered a rapist and possible murderer. Evil can't live in His Presence.

Day-stars

In my own life so much goodness, so much fulfillment, so much to be thankful for . . . A deeper dimension to my prayers, a warmer, dearer, surer relationship with people . . .

Lord, why then the little inner river of restlessness? The sense of something still lacking?

I had so much already, yes. My friend was right—I probably didn't need it. Not now that I had the substance, the nourishing substance . . . But I yearned for the sweet as well!

I wanted your song. I wanted the reward. I wanted the thrill of your voice mingling with mine. I wanted the deep inner peace and the outward radiance that I saw in those who had received.

I wanted the protection you gave my daughter that night.

"All right, so I'm a coward," I admitted to you, God. "Please forgive my cowardice and my pride. Show me, shake me, take me, give me the courage to do whatever must be done. . . .

"If you really want me to keep on bearing witness to it, give me the secret, God."

Then one day alone at our country cabin on the lake . . . A beautiful day. Nobody else about. I had a sense of some fateful appointment. *Today?* a small voice seemed to be asking. And the answer could not be denied—*Today. . . . Now? . . . As soon as you're ready.* Something both merry and tender brushed my heart. I thought of John. (*You're ready now, John.*)

I poured another cup of coffee, read on awhile in my accumulation of books and articles by people so eager to share, to help me. I browsed again through Frances Hunter's book *The Two Sides to a Coin,* wherein she describes her progress from outright hostility for tongues to glorious conversion, when she simply dared to *try.* . . . I leafed through one of half a dozen Bibles in various translations. In the early stages of my interest I had begun marking with a yellow highlighter pen every reference I found to the Holy Ghost or Spirit. It was like lighting little bonfires in the Bible, especially in the New Testament—they blazed from almost every page!

I remembered Hope's words earlier, and read them for myself now as Peter expressed them in Acts 2: ". . . and ye shall receive the gift of the Holy Ghost. For the promise is unto you, and to your children, and to all that are afar off, even as many as the Lord our God shall call."

I had read them many times before, but today they spoke to *me.* There, in black and white, shining from my own pen's underscoring, was the promise. A promise already realized by one of my children. Now it was indeed as if the Lord was calling one of those "afar off."

I arose and went out onto the balcony. Had I been stalling? Was I still afraid? Of what? That it might not happen? Or that it *might?* Did I really want what I claimed I sought?

Overhead the sky was a vivid cloudless blue, marked only by a white heron that came gliding toward the water, and a lazily circling hawk. Below, the lake was a broad silver mirror reflecting in absolute perfection the lovely sky and the leaning green trees. But when a little wind stirred its surface it exploded with a myriad of blazing sun-stars.

I felt like that—at peace with God. As if I'd grown beyond my own stormy waters, and now my life could reflect, if not with perfection, some of the beauty I had found. But I still wanted to explode, burst forth with the sparkling glory of those dancing day-stars.

"Please, Lord, help me. If I make a fool of myself, so be it—I'm going to *try!*" And with a fleeting glance around to make sure nobody was near, I lifted my arms, let my tongue go, deliberately uttering a syllable or two, then a consciously fashioned word. . . . And suddenly a fountain of words was gushing from me, bright as those ever-changing day-stars.

Strange words . . . beautiful words . . . accompanied by a feeling of sheer rapture. It was happening, it was happening! and tears of joy ran down my face.

It was worship of the purest, most enthralling kind. It was also a total unleashing and surrender of all my soul's concerns. I was conscious of my family and all the people I care about, without having to articulate their needs. . . . I was conscious of a great inner purging and imploring I had never been quite able to express. I realized now the true significance of the passage: "Likewise the Spirit also helpeth our infirmities: for we know not what we should pray for as we ought: but the Spirit itself maketh intercession for us with groanings which cannot be uttered" (Rom. 8:26).

I went indoors and got down on my knees. . . . I turned on some music and danced as I prayed. . . . The lovely language continued to pour forth for hours. All that morning, in my sunny solitude, I prayed.

And I realized what Jesus meant when he said we must be born again of the water *and of the Spirit* if we are truly to enter the kingdom of God. . . . All this time! . . . I didn't feel I'd been *outside* the kingdom, no, for the kingdom is vast. But I had been circling, circling, wanting to draw nearer, ever nearer to the palace gates. Now the gates had been flung wide. I had entered the very heart of the kingdom.

Why did I wait so long, Lord? Why did I wait so long even to try?
Like so many things in life we keep putting off, even when the inner self keeps urging, why did I wait so long simply to reach out and release those golden gates?

The Same Yesterday, Today and Forever

I must deal with some of the objections I will hear.

I will ask God to help me. And I realize he has already given me the most dependable evidence I can possibly have—his Word. Anyone can find the right answers there. Anyone who will go to the Bible as I did and search out every reference to the Spirit or Holy Ghost and mark it in yellow will find it lighting up. Like little signal fires throughout the Old Testament . . . and the New suddenly ablaze!

Now divorce yourself from man-made doctrine, forget all the

stock dismissals, negations, explanations and assumptions you've
ever heard. Bring your mind clear and clean to the Gospels and listen with your own ears to what they say.

Now ask yourself why, if this Baptism in the Spirit was so vital
that Jesus himself spoke of it often and held it out as the supreme
gift to be bestowed upon his followers . . . why, if he commanded
that they ready themselves to receive it, and accept it as the *sign* of
the Comforter's return . . . why, if it did indeed confirm his promise
and gave them the will and fervor to go out and preach and heal
and save—gave them even the courage to die for him . . . why, if
this marvelous power and blessing existed at all, it should have been
arbitrarily wiped out of existence when the last word in the book was
written and the covers attached?

If it was a sign of their faith, why not ours? If it was a commandment to them, why not us? If they were exhorted to go forth and
proclaim it, share it, help others to receive it, why shouldn't we?
Aren't we also disciples of Christ and children of God? Aren't we
also desperately in need of faith and power and the strength to overcome? . . . And aren't all the commandments of Jesus as valid today as the moment he gave them? "Jesus Christ the same yesterday,
and to day, and for ever" (Heb. 13:8).

Dare we pick and choose which of his orders we shall honor and
which refuse? Dare we scorn and scoff at or even ignore the Holy
Ghost? The one of whom Jesus said, in no uncertain terms: "All
manner of sin and blasphemy shall be forgiven unto men: but the
blasphemy against the Holy Ghost shall not be forgiven . . ." (Matt.
12:31).

Are we not to follow, insofar as we humanly can, Jesus' own example? His forerunner, John the Baptist, proclaimed: ". . . one mightier than I cometh . . . he shall baptize you with the Holy Ghost . . ."
(Luke 3:16).

Jesus himself was baptized, first with water, then the Spirit:
". . . Jesus also being baptized, and praying, the heaven was
opened, And the Holy Ghost descended in a bodily shape like a dove
upon him . . ." (Luke 3:21–22).

It was the Spirit that led him into the wilderness immediately
thereafter and sustained him through his first temptation: "And
Jesus being full of the Holy Ghost returned from Jordan, and was
led by the Spirit into the wilderness. . . . And when the devil had
ended all the temptation, he departed from him for a season. And

Jesus returned in the power of the Spirit into Galilee" (Luke 4:1, 13–14).

For his first recorded sermon in the Nazareth synagogue he chose his text from the prophet Esaias, where it was written: "The Spirit of the Lord is upon me, because he hath anointed me to preach . . ." (Luke 4:18).

Throughout his ministry he performed miracles through the power of his father, whom he called spirit, and spoke repeatedly of the need to be born again and to drink the spiritual waters: "If any man thirst, let him come unto me, and drink. He that believeth on me, as the scripture hath said, out of his belly shall flow rivers of living water. (But this spake he of the Spirit, which they that believe on him should receive: for the Holy Ghost was not yet given . . .)" (John 7:37–39).

In his farewell sermon (the one that begins "Let not your heart be troubled") he emphasized the coming of the Comforter. Not once but three times the promise was made (John 14:26; 15:26; 16:7)! And how poignant the passage: "But the Comforter, which is the Holy Ghost, whom the Father will send in my name, he shall teach you all things, and bring all things to your remembrance, whatsoever I have said unto you" (John 14:26).

He wanted them to remember him and do what he said. The Comforter not only would assure this, but would continue to teach them. And his final admonition to them, after the resurrection and just before the ascension, was: "Receive ye the Holy Ghost" (John 20:22).

Aren't we supposed to remember him, too, and follow him, and learn? Was the Comforter only for *them?*

It seems to me incredible that churches still include the Trinity in their doctrine and even baptize "In the name of the Father, and of the Son, and of the Holy Ghost" if the third person of the Trinity has been denuded of all significance. And particularly if any manifestation of his actual working presence in lives today is regarded as false or threatening.

The Holy Ghost was the most important fact in the life of the early church, from the day of Pentecost on through the final Revelations. There are far too many incidents and references to the Baptism in the Spirit to cite here. But to be filled with the Spirit, speak the language of the Spirit, use the gifts of the Spirit, was to them an absolute sign of conversion and the presence of Christ. And that it was glowing, exciting, power-giving, miracle-working, soul-winning, and unifying is plain.

A common objection: "It can divide a church."

Church dividings have been going on for years. (The church of my childhood split up three times.) Over buildings and missionaries and preachers some faction doesn't like, over social issues and a dozen other things. Yet we don't stop building or sending out missionaries nor fire all the clergy. The church survives.

And why should a church—a *church* of all things—be scared and go to pieces over a resurrection, especially of the *Holy Ghost?* One of its own foundation premises! Not that all churches have to become charismatic or change their mode of worship in any way. But the presence of even a few spirit-filled Christians ought to be a joyous, regenerating influence instead of a threat.

Another objection: "People who receive the Baptism and speak in tongues feel superior." . . . I have never known a Spirit-filled Christian who didn't feel so humble and so blessed he wanted everybody to have the same experience.

And: "The devil can duplicate the phenomenon."

Yes, the devil is clever. He can also sing in the choir, pass the collection plate, and preach eloquent sermons. But we don't forgo these things for fear of being duped. We go on trusting God and using an infallible test the Lord gave us: "By their fruits ye shall know them." People who are truly baptized in the Spirit are able to throw off habits that may have shackled them for years. They witness for Jesus in a way more staid believers fear to, and they often heal. Some of them have put their lives on the line in working with desperate people, particularly drug addicts. David Wilkerson and Arthur Blessitt are just two of thousands. The results the Holy Spirit has obtained through them are phenomenal.

In any case, the reborn Christian is happier, more charitable, truly regenerated in every aspect of his being. He sings "A New Song," as Pat Boone puts it. And it's beautiful!

To long to love God and to know him better. To hunger for that closeness with a hunger that can't be explained . . . And to have the very touchstone to his spirit so available . . .

But don't listen to me, listen to the Lord himself.

Go to the Bible. Look, look—and listen!

Loving

But the greatest of these is love.

1 Corinthians 13:13

No Limits On Love

Who are you, God? Where are you? How do I find you? How can I truly know you?

The heavens declare your glory, the whole world is witness to your wonders. I find you in nature, in birth and death and the very pain that is my lot. All beauty speaks to me of you, all the creative arts. And I can speak to you through prayer; your own Holy Spirit responds.

Yet one thing more I must have truly to be one with you. And that is love. . . . Yes, of course I love, or these things would not have meaning. But if I am to merge deeply with your being I must love more. Not just wind and water and stars and sky because they are of you; not merely my work or books and music and painting, not even my times of prayer. I must love my fellow human beings.

Oh, but I do, I do! I insist. . . . And your voice seems to ask: "How much? Enough to refrain from hurting? Enough to forgive? Enough to sacrifice, to serve, to rescue? Do you really love your neighbor as yourself?"

I can only whimper—I try, I'm trying. After all, I'm only human, and there are so many demands. There are limits on my energy, my time, my money, my strength. Limits on—my love!

And God seems to reply: "There are no limits on love."

No limits on his love—no. (For God is omnipotent, and God is love.) But how about mine? I am not God, far from it. I am a weak, faulty person. I get busy and angry, hold grudges sometimes; I blurt out words that hurt, words I regret. I do my best to help people but I can't help everyone—every neighbor who gets sick, needs a baby-sitter or a willing shoulder to cry on, every writer who presents me with a manuscript. (How would I take care of my own family, how would I get my own writing done?) Yet they tug at my heart, all these needs on my own doorstep . . . As for the needs of the world! I can't contribute to every cause, however worthy (so many it's hard

even to know what the worthy ones *are*) . . . As for the world's
poor—

The raggedy children in Israel, swarming around every tourist.
Hands open for begging, or filled with cheap trinkets to sell—
olivewood rosaries, strings of carved camels and donkeys. To give to
one or buy from one is to be besieged. I had to flee from one little
mob who had literally attacked. Scared? yes, but oddly not angry.
Too hurt to be angry, hurt by their haunted faces, the anguish of
the poverty that set them on "a rich American." Stricken at my utter
helplessness before such need.

*No limits on love . . . Is that what you mean, Lord? Even power-
less and frightened I could still love those children. For you place no
limits on love.*

Thinking of that, I feel better. God, in his infinite understanding,
knows our limitations. Of time, money, physical strength. He expects
us to do what we can (and it's really quite a lot) but only what we
can. He makes allowances for all that we fail to accomplish, so long
as we love.

That is the secret, just to love. . . . But when we *can* help, *do*
help, then we are quick with his living presence. And there is no joy
like it.

To Love as a Little Child

Children realize this, as they sense so much else that is really important. We hear that children are cruel and selfish—and observing
them banging each other over the head or struggling for a toy it
seems that way. But we overlook the many instances when they rush
to each other's aid. . . . A toddler falls out of his wagon, and a sister
not much bigger rushes to his howling side. "I help you, honey," she
soothes. And she struggles to pick him up and lug him to Mother for
mending.

Or another small child will press upon his contemporaries a lolli-
pop, a box of crayons, a flower. Or they labor in ecstatic secrecy over
surprises for a parent, a teacher, anyone they love.

Christmas. Walk along any city street with a mittened hand in
yours. Hear the Salvation Army bells ringing above the sound of
carols and the babble of busy shoppers. You've already made your

contribution, you try to hasten past the booth, but the child pulls back. "Wait, I gotta put something in the kettle." Clutching his last coins, he marches proudly forward. "Thank you, God bless you," the bonneted lady smiles. He returns, face shining, God-touched.

Appeal to any Cub or Brownie troop for help—stuffing stockings for orphanages, making cookies and carrying them to shut-ins, or helping with a needy family. They go crazy with love, bounce with love, vie to do the most, make the most, give the most. Want to take on more than you had bargained for—they recognize no limits on love. . . .

Or turn to any young people's group—fraternity, sorority, club—if you need help cleaning up flats in a ghetto or raising funds for the victims of famine or flood. They will march, canvass, slave. For every one out to rob, hurt, or destroy there are five hundred with hammers in hand to build, and the Lord's own stars in their eyes.

Or at home, among your own. Though they try to groan out of requests to rake the yard or scrub a floor, they leap to the challenge of helping outsiders. . . . What Christmases will my children most vividly remember? "The year we made the Raggedy Anns and Andys for the Doll House to give away." "The years we adopted the Wilsons and the Kelseys—" The sixth-grader herself suggested that project. A classmate's family "adopted another family for Christmas, why can't we?" Oh no, please, I'm already swamped! I mentally implored. But the Lord gives you strength. And we mended and baked and shopped and refurbished toys. And sitting around our own tree Christmas Eve, its lights shone more brightly knowing that in another otherwise cold house there was warmth and a shining tree, and gifts to greet the morning.

Yes, the carols and the candles and the words at the midnight service brought you close, dear Lord. But the real joy, the real love we felt for you and for each other lay in this deep sweet knowledge.

The Beautiful People

Who are the beautiful people in this world? The truly beautiful people? In the captious games we play with language we've pinned this label on what we also call the Jet Set. International playboys and girls, rich and often famous, who yacht or jet around the world entertaining each other. Are these people happy? Since I don't know any of them personally—can only read about their divorces and dazzling doings and affairs or see them on TV—who am I to judge?

But I do know a lot of genuinely beautiful people who are surely the happiest people on earth. People who live lives of total love, whose religion is total service. We call them the Salvation Army. And if I want a glimpse of God I have only to look at their faces. . . . Read God there—laughing on their lips, sparkling from their eyes. Observe how lightly and surely they move in their proud but simple uniforms; they work among the poor, yes, but they live in the Kingdom of Heaven.

Talk about the joy of doing something for others at Christmas—they are celebrating Christmas every day! And even those who associate with such people are brushed by their magic dust. I sometimes think of the Salvation Army as a benevolent parent who not only shields and shepherds the needy, but whose arms reach out to include the countless volunteers who gain so much by giving.

Jesus said, "Inasmuch as ye have done it unto one of the least of these my brethren, ye have done it unto me." And, "Eye hath not seen, nor ear heard, . . . the things which God hath prepared for them that love him." *That* is their secret. And whenever I hear people bemoaning their loneliness or lacks I want to protest (and do): "Oh, stop looking in, start looking out!" For there's no city so large or village so small there aren't people much worse off. His brethren, and ours, in desperate need of us . . . Yes, you. Yes, me. And in helping them, joining forces with others to help them, we can find outlet for our energies, surcease from our own problems, and a unique and vital companionship.

It needn't be the Salvation Army—any group of concerned volunteers. . . . But my beloved Army, here in Washington, D.C. All year groups of people unconnected with the Army meet to dress dolls for little girls they'll never see. Government secretaries, telephone operators, clerks, nurses. And back of the placards when the dolls are displayed lie hours of fun and satisfaction as busy people forgot themselves after a long hard day. . . . Santa's Workshop, where women are stuffing stockings. Clatter of staplers and tongues. A spill of small toys on the table . . . the smell of coffee, the comradeship.

And the Toy Center, some vacant building a generous businessman donates every year. Here the mountains of bulging stockings, and the ranks of dolls beaming row on row. And hundreds of new toys to be given to decent, dignified parents who simply couldn't provide Christmas for their children any other way. And helping to fill their shopping bags, wrap the larger presents, provide a word of cheer, are women and sometimes husbands, and often daughters and tall young sons. (And the years my own daughter came along to work beside me were the sweetest, most Christ-conscious years of all.) People with families or people without any family. But all busily involved in something as warm and shining as the lights on the ceiling-high tree.

And backstage, men from the Harbor Light (the Army's sanctuary for men who need help) eagerly working, checking lights, putting up shelves, hauling and uncrating the gifts, replenishing the supply of hot coffee . . . and co-ordinating all this an unsung saint, Florence Goins, who's been doing it for nearly twenty years—"In memory of my mother. She belonged to the regular Army and this project was so dear to her. Just before she died she asked, 'One of you girls will continue my Toy Shop, won't you?' I told her, 'Mother, I will do it every year so long as I am alive.' And each year as I enter, I tell her, 'Here I am, Mother, keeping your wish again.' And when I go out the door—'Mother, dear, I have fulfilled your wish once more.' "

And when the excitement is over these quiet people attend to the least inspiring job of all, the clearing out and cleaning up.

Christmas is but one colorful aspect of the work of this mighty army. We become especially aware of it at the season when the Holy Spirit wants our hearts to echo "Good will to men." But throughout the year these beautiful people are activating the entire parable: "For I was an hungred, and ye gave me meat: I was thirsty, and ye gave me drink: I was a stranger, and ye took me in: Naked, and ye clothed me: I was sick and ye visited me: I was in prison, and ye came unto me" (Matt. 25:35–36).

The Saints Unsung

The Quiet People. The saints unsung. You don't have to relate to a group to relate to God through loving and giving. You can do it alone (or almost alone). You can do it without drives or money. *Guideposts* magazine has a series called just that, "The Quiet Peo-

ple." About individuals who devote their time and energy to making
life brighter for others:

Seventy-year-old Herb Besant, who builds elaborate birdhouses
and gives them away to shut-ins. (Two hundred so far.) "You've no
idea of the joy that old people, who spend their entire day looking
out a window, get out of a birdhouse and the birds that come to it."

Henry Perry, "The guy who lends the bikes." Figuring most poor
kids who steal bikes only want to ride, he began assembling and re-
pairing unwanted bikes for them to borrow. "Word spread and
thirty or forty lined up waiting their turn." Now they help fix them,
and he has a bike drill team. . . .

Loraine Miller, unmarried schoolteacher, who for forty years has
been investing in needy college students. At first ten dollars a month,
then letters, clothes, visits. Of the seventeen she has helped put
through college, five are clergymen (including James Robinson,
whose African example helped inspire the Peace Corps); six are
teachers, one a lawyer, three are serving in Africa; another, a uni-
versity professor, is establishing educational systems in African
countries. ("Divide and multiply!")

Albert Rosen, a Jew who began standing in for Christians who
had to work Christmas Eve. His wife joined him; and ultimately all
three hundred members of his synagogue. Then Christian groups
reciprocated, so their Jewish brothers and sisters were free to worship on their holy days. Now it's become a community project.
"Kindness is contagious," he says. But, like the Salvation Army, it
isn't just once a year he proves his God is love. He corresponds with
prisoners, regularly visits inmates, and helps them find jobs when
they get out. . . .

The list is endless. And my own list of quiet unsung saints . . .
Mac and Helen, for instance. Jon and Morrell. Neighbors when we
first moved to Washington. Same church, same coping with kids. So
good, so generous, so much fun, and bubbling with the joy of a love
that knows no limits . . . Both houses always aswarm with relatives,
strangers, foreign students, the ill, the lonely, anybody who needed
a nest. Forever rushing to people's rescue, transporting people to
hospitals, airports, schools. Forever loading cars with old people who
needed to get out, or food and clothing for hard-hit families.

As for their friends . . . My husband's heart attack, long after
we'd moved to separate suburbs. Winter, and the doctor said to

recuperate in the South, away from the cold. Impossible for us both to go, we still had a child in school. . . . Then the delegation appeared. "Now you're going, we've got it all worked out. We'll take turns keeping her and getting her to school." And they did, though it meant a daily round trip of fifty miles. What's more, after two weeks they wired us, "Stay the rest of the month!"

Now why do people do such things? Why do they give up their own time, spend their own money, put themselves to so much trouble? Because God is love. And God implanted in every breast this living, throbbing life line to each other and to him: the ability to love each other. And when we grab that life line and throw it to each other, then we invigorate and strengthen our thrilling connection with God.

The Bible says, "Faith without works is dead." We can't and don't love God unless we love each other enough to do those works. But what about works without faith? What about the fine and generous people who do good works and yet claim they don't believe in God? Well, okay, God believes in *them*. Let the mind refuse to acknowledge its own Creator; the spirit pays no attention. It goes right on loving God and doing his bidding. That's what God sees. Not the resistant, rationalizing mind, only the loving spirit.

The pity is that such people miss the abundance, the overflowing joy that comes when our life line stretches beyond us—just us and those we are able to help—and soars right up to the God we serve.

Margaret

The nicest people seem to bear the same names. There have been two Hopes in my life, each with the shining qualities of that symbolic name. . . . Two Evelyns, two Elizabeths, and two Margarets. Every one of them high on my list of unsung saints . . .

The two Margarets:

My husband's sister Margaret, who would literally sell what she has and give to the poor if we didn't restrain her. Whose greatest pleasure in life is giving, whose only grief is that she can't give more. Why does she enjoy sharing all she has so much? Because it never occurs to her to take credit. It's all God's anyway, isn't it? she reasons. . . .

And that other Margaret—Margaret Simpson—who began to

write to me shortly after the publication of *I've Got to Talk to Somebody, God*. Wife of a banker in Eufaula, a small town not far from Tulsa. Sunday school teacher, lay witness, speaker; counseling, comforting, doing every kind of handwork and heartwork known to woman. And rejoicing, that is the main thing, continually astonished at the blessings that rain down in triple return. I must quote from some of her letters:

If only I could give you, by the process of osmosis, some of my precious moments with God so you could write them for me (much of the time I feel I'm going to spill over!).

I have been asked to speak in two churches in April while the ministers are on vacation. I think I will call my talk Show and Tell. About being willing to make oneself vulnerable for God— giving a part of oneself in order to give God's joy and agapé to others . . . One example will be a woman who has given me a special part in her redeemed life, though I have never seen her. Periodically she calls me asking for advice and prayers. Linda has been a dope addict, alcoholic, in a mental hospital, in prison. Married five or six times, she has seven children and is raising a child of a fellow prisoner. Her life is being straightened out with the help of God; however, as a result of her past, her children have many problems. Though I have many sins of the spirit I have not experienced any of these problems, and it is a mystery how I am used to help her. It has to be of God. . . .

I feel that many things in my life are the result of proddings from the Holy Spirit because of a prayer—"What do you want me to do for you today, God?" One had just better not say that unless it is sincere, because he will for sure give you something to do. What is so very remarkable is that I am the one who gets the blessing, quadrupled, pressed down and running over, and flowing on and on.

Oh the WONDER of God! How, how can I tell the stories of how the tiny sincere bits of myself, given to those whose actions touch me so deeply within my soul, come back to me increased? How can it be told with modesty and humility to cause others to want to give themselves—to "Show and Tell" God's love? NOT to get something BACK, but just for the joy of loving and doing and being for GOD!

In another letter she has just come from a visit to Curt, a seventeen-year-old in jail. She told me his story—beaten repeatedly by a stepfather, kicked out at fifteen, desperate and in trouble with the law. She had gotten permission to visit him, take him books and magazines since he loved to read. And write! "I hate to impose, but some of his poems seem remarkable for anyone his age. Could you possibly take time to tell me frankly what you think?" I read them open-mouthed, then had to wipe my eyes. Out of this tormented boy had come such beautiful things I published them in my column.

Margaret wrote back, ecstatic. "This may change his life. It's the first recognition he's ever had from anyone. At least now he knows someone else believes in him!"

Again, she enclosed a picture of a forlorn little boy, dirty, neglected, head buried in his arms as he crouched on the steps of a tenement: "I came across this picture of this little child whose utter hopelessness, hurt and aloneness filled me with such compassion that for a few seconds I was one with Christ and could understand his willingness to give his life for me. . . ."

This strikes home. Hard. No, finding God through loving is not all joy, far from it. Pain is very much a part of it. It makes me vulnerable. I cannot ignore the cross of another; even if I am powerless to lift it, I stagger with the weight of it on my heart.

No, no, please! My own cross is heavy, there are lashes on my back, too, I've got wounds of my own to heal.

Give me the joy of helping, Lord, spare me the hurting. Especially when I can't help . . . Then I remember your words: "Blessed are the merciful."

And I know that without mercy, whatever its cost, I can't love either God or man.

Two by the Side of the Road

Mercy. Inseparable from love. At least in the eyes of God. I look in my concordance for the word *mercy* in all its forms. I look there for the word *love*. To my surprise they occupy equal space. The Bible speaks of mercy as often as it does of love!

Mercy. Compassion. Kindness. "Love suffereth long, and is kind."

Impossible then to love anyone or anything without this kindness. Cruelty has no place in love. If you love an animal you cannot be cruel to it (at least without awful remorse). Or intentionally cruel to the mate or child you love. I heard someone say: "He hurts the most the ones he loves the most." "On purpose?" "Sure, all the time. He enjoys it. But later he's usually sorry."

This isn't God's kind of love, it can't be. It's a distortion of love. A sado-masochistic self-love masquerading. Genuine love wants to relieve pain, not inflict it. And when the demons in us take over (as they often do), when we say or do cruel things to those we love, then our own suffering later may surpass theirs. . . . This remorse, this awful devastation—isn't it the stern side of God showing us that cruelty has no place in love?

Only mercy. Compassion. Understanding . . . To identify. Empathize. To know how hurting *feels* . . . Do unto others as ye would have them do unto you.

And this identification extends beyond those close to you. It includes that poor kid scribbling his poems on grubby envelopes in prison, and even the *picture* of an abandoned child. . . . It makes you one with every individual whose need you see. A swift and poignant merging so that you *are* that person for an instant. Even that insecure stranger at the party, nervously hoping someone will speak to him. Because you know how it feels (and can't stand how it feels) you go to him, hand outstretched. . . . You *are* that suffering patient on a stretcher, or the distraught man or woman standing by. And the hurt is too much, you've got to do something to assuage it, if only by an encouraging word,

Jesus, dear Jesus, I sometimes envy you! When you felt pity for people you had only to reach out and touch them and they were healed. You could make them walk again, you could restore their sight. . . . I feel such pity for people, but so helpless before their plight. Jesus, dear Jesus, show me what to do.

The Good Samaritan. That parable was for all of us. That parable was for me. . . . Oh, but it takes courage to be a Good Samaritan, it can look silly, even be dangerous. It's not safe to go to anybody's rescue any more, not even by daylight on a busy street. New York, especially. People don't pay any attention, just walk on by.

And I'm in New York now, taking a walk before a luncheon appointment, on a bitterly cold day. And across the street, in front of
a funeral home, lies a body. Heavens, don't they even pick up their
bodies? Don't look, none of your business, hurry on by. . . . But
what if—? Never mind, look in store windows, beautiful clothes,
forget that—*but what if it isn't a body?* None of your business,
don't be a hick. . . . Okay, okay, cross the street, walk back just to
be sure, it's probably gone by now. . . . Only it isn't, and people
are stepping around it, paying no attention, although you see it
moving, hear its feeble cries—"Help me . . . some-body!" Okay,
okay, hick, chicken out-of-towner, break down, make a fool of yourself, ask what's the matter?

He's shaking, haggard, sick. He needs food, something warm in
his stomach. If you give him some money will he please go in out of
the cold and eat? (You are begging for yourself!) He agrees, sobbing, and you hand him a dollar, escape. (Fool, he'll use it for
drink.) When you look back he waves so plaintively you can't
stand it. So *go* back, *go* back, idiot. "Your problem is alcohol, isn't
it? Will you go to A.A. if I can get you there? They'll help you."

"Lady . . . I'll go . . . anywhere!"

Try to find a phone booth, try to find their number. They say
they can't come after him, but if I can bring him by taxi . . . Try to
get a taxi. . . . He is sitting up now, and another woman has
stopped to talk to him. "Would you like for me to go with you?" she
asks. Thank God. Especially since the headquarters prove to be in
an undesirable section. (Could you have gotten him safely up those
stairs by yourself, hick? Would the cab driver, sweet guy that he
seemed to be, have helped you?) No matter, the other Good Samaritan supports his other side. . . . And they welcome him kindly, assure us he will have medical attention, food, a bed.

Leaving, the woman and I agree we, too, will sleep better to-
night, knowing that. And that we could use some coffee ourselves.
"He was worth saving," she says. "He's an educated man—did you
notice his diction? And his manners, even so sick. When he said he'd
never forget us he meant it. He's a good but very sick man."

Belatedly, we exchange names—and gasp. She is Ann Williams-
Heller, well-known nutritionist. She writes for the same magazines
I do, knows the same people! We fall into each other's arms, friends.
. . . She came to this country as an Austrian war refugee. Now,

years later, love brought us together. Out of all the people swarming the New York streets, the same life line from the same God drew us together at the side of someone who was suffering.

". . . whatsoever good thing any man doeth, the same shall he receive of the Lord. . . ."

It's not always that swift, that clear. Now I must record the incident of the old woman in Haifa, not to exalt myself, heaven knows, but only to try to understand the peculiar anguish of another love shared. . . .

She was bent over, heavy and stooped, with a homemade crutch under one arm, and in the other hand a knobby stick on which to lean. At her feet, a string bag filled with groceries. Evidently she had been shopping and discovered she could not carry them. She was weeping and making pitiful gestures to people thrusting past on the steep hot street.

I halted, torn. Our bus was making only a brief stop. Long enough to explore some of the art shops. I was rushing up the hill to look at some mosaics glimpsed in a window. But my heart would not let me pass. I halted, picked up the heavy bag, and tried to walk with her a little way.

Then I saw that her poor old feet in their run-over shoes could scarcely make it. She had to pause every few inches and point to one of them, so swollen it had broken through the thin flopping slipper. I set down the bag and knelt to examine it; the shoe was so broken and dusty it had rubbed the flesh raw. How to help, what to do? I tried putting a Kleenex in the sole to ease it a little bit. I caressed her foot with my fingers. Then I stood up and said, "Lean on me." And thus we progressed a little way.

Meanwhile, I was trying to enlist the aid of an Israeli soldier—anyone who might know where she lived and come to her aid. But if they understood they gave no sign; they simply shrugged and went on. All I could do was talk to her encouragingly in a language she did not understand. And when she had to stop again the hurt was too much for both of us, the love; I embraced her and kissed her and we clung together, so at least she realized that somebody cared. And she gazed at me through her tragic old eyes beneath the ragged shawl, and the tears flowed afresh.

The others were returning to the bus, calling, "Come on!" I would have to leave her. In desperation I hailed a boy of about fifteen and pleaded, "Do you speak English? Do you know where this woman lives? Can't you please carry her things home?" To my relief, he nodded, took up the bag, and set off down the hill. Behind him she continued to plod, inching along, halted again and again by the agonies of age. The last I saw was that stooped figure still making its tortuous way downhill in the blazing sun.

And my heart cried out after her. I felt as if I was abandoning her, as if I ought to give up all the comforts and joys of my own life to make her life easier . . . in that awful moment of recognition she was my mother! She was all the mothers who have borne children and grown old and crippled and live in poverty and torment as they struggle through their final days. I wanted to help her. I wanted to know that she lay on clean sheets in a cool house with somebody nearby to soothe her and keep her company.

I wanted to heal her. And to be able to do so little hurt so much.

I said that I sometimes envy Jesus. Now I realize . . . he couldn't heal everyone either, he couldn't provide for all the poor. There were simply too many. He, too, was limited by time and energy. And if *he* had limitations, how much greater are my human limitations. And if I suffer because of them, how much more he must have suffered for those people he had to turn away. (And must suffer still for us.)

But this I must remember. There were and are no limits on his love. All he asks of me is that I put no limits on my love.

With the Tongues of Men and Angels

Jesus said: "Thou shalt love the Lord thy God with all thy heart, and with all thy soul, and with all thy mind. That is the first and great commandment. And the second is like unto it, Thou shalt love thy neighbor as thyself."

The thirteenth chapter of First Corinthians tells us how. The famous chapter on charity, or love. And how that Paul could write! No author, not even Shakespeare, has ever produced anything to surpass that treatise. "Though I speak with the tongues of men and of angels, and have not love, I am become as sounding brass, or a tinkling cymbal."

Read it, oh read it to learn the true nature of love. Some versions use the word *charity;* no matter, the words are interchangeable, they mean the same thing. (And how significant that is.) Generosity, giving, sharing, having mercy, being patient, showing compassion, understanding. And no matter what I say, or how many people I help, if I go about this bitterly or grudgingly, then "it profiteth me nothing." If I am truly to know and love God, I must have love for his people in my heart.

This means I will be charitable in my spirit as well as my acts. I will refrain from judgments. ("Judge not, that ye be not judged. . . ." Who knows what agony lies behind the locked doors of another person's life?) I will not stone a brother or sister with words. ("Inasmuch as ye have done it unto one of the least of these my brethren, ye have done it unto me.")

I will love my neighbors, and show it whenever I can even though I may not tell them so. I will try to love my God with all my heart and soul and mind—and *tell* him so.

For the very words of love enhance and intensify love. If I want to find God and hang on to him, I've got to thank him for creating me and letting me live. Every moment of my life will be a witness to that wonder. But he will be closer, ever closer, if I love him and tell him so!

"And now abideth all these things . . ." that have helped lead me back to God.

People and writings and work. Birth and death and nature. The church and prayer and pain and the wonders of art.

"*. . . but the greatest of these is love.*"